"Those involved in leading large organizations—or those who aspire to lead—may never encounter an organization-threatening crisis. But for those who do, their ability to lead their organization out of the valley of crisis will be the critical event by which, when all is said and done, their careers will be measured. Ignore this story at your peril!"

—John Graham Cook
Retired VP HR, Fortune 400 Corporation

"*Powerful.* Hutson and Johnson's practical, hard-hitting insights about crisis show that our best laid plans may only work for the crises that we anticipate. The accelerating storm of technological, economic, and social upheaval will test today's executives like no generation before. *Navigating an Organizational Crisis* is required reading for executives who don't want to be overwhelmed by wave after wave of inevitable disruption."

—John M. Dillard
Author of *Microslices: The Death of Consulting and What It Means for Executives*
and President of Big Sky Associates

"Anyone charged with leadership or aspiring to it will find wisdom and inspiration here. *Navigating an Organizational Crisis* rings with insight and authenticity."

—David Dodson
President, MDC
Durham, North Carolina

"Take it from me, real leadership is never an easy ride. There are pearls of wisdom in this book that continue to be helpful to me as a leader, though one in particular stands out: be a listener, a good listener, even when you don't like what you're hearing."

—Michael Dukakis
Former Governor of Massachusetts

"Harry Hutson and Martha Johnson's *Navigating an Organizational Crisis* provides an important corrective to the cheery optimism of the modern self-help literature. The authors insist that leaders inevitably experience crises, change, and pain—even as they are entrusted with the livelihood of others. The authenticity, grit, and compassion with which they handle their personal and organizational difficulties, not their obvious successes, may be the greatest measures of their mettle. Resilience, not will power, is the gateway to the type of personal transformation sought by the authors."

—Barry Dym, PhD
President and CEO
Institute for Nonprofit Management and Leadership

"For today's leader, the rogue wave event is unexpected but inevitable. Hutson and Johnson's penetrating perspective provides footing and direction for self, colleagues, and the entire organization in weathering the unforeseen. I found their demonstration of the use of stories in leading the way to recovery, renewal, and growth to be especially powerful and useful."

—John Furcon
Director, Research & Consulting
Northwestern University Center for Public Safety

"The captain and crew navigating rogue waves—the metaphor could not be more apt! Harry and Martha's research is solid and the storytelling poignant—should be a primer for all leaders. They show that the fundamentals of leadership, especially in a crisis, are the same and scalable whether in the private or public sector. Wonderful!"

—John A. Glowacki Jr.
COO, Shared Services Canada;
Former CTO, Computer Sciences Corp.

"The authors add a new dimension to the field of crisis management, providing an emotional framework to assist leaders who must navigate through crisis situations. They bring the five elements of their framework to life with excellent examples of leaders who are reflecting, reaching for help, responding, restoring through story telling, and seeking renewal in crisis situations. Their chapter on the power of 'story telling' is highly relevant to all leaders in all leadership situations."

—William K. Hall
Adjunct Professor at the University of Michigan
and Private Equity/ Venture Capital Investor in Chicago

"*Navigating an Organizational Crisis* does something remarkable by frankly discussing what actually happens when the world goes topsy-turvy and we recognize that we must lead, our organization must respond, and the moment is now! Through their research on leaders in crisis, Harry and Martha reveal important insights that guide and inform new and experienced leaders. By shining a bright light into leadership's dark corners, they help us see the world as it is—unpredictable—and help each of us grasp the value of leadership—our leadership—through attention, compassion, and pragmatic choice."

—Rob Hartz
Leader, Leadership Facilitator, Executive Coach

"How does an individual prevail against insurmountable forces? The answer lies in the stories recounted here. Hutson and Johnson describe the walls of water and fire confronting contemporary Americans who were able to summon extraordinary inner strengths to navigate and weather their ordeals. Theirs is a collective story of resourcefulness, resilience, and renewal."

—Richard S. Jerauld, MD

"Today's complex, dynamic workplace heightens the likelihood of a leader facing unexpected calamity. Hutson and Johnson's book fills a gap in the leadership literature by giving actionable insight to successfully navigating organizational catastrophe and thereby discovering meaning, purpose, hope, and especially humanity. The baseness of unforeseen crisis can be transformed into golden growth, creating leadership alchemy."

—Ann-Marie Johnson
Founder
NeoBridge

"Superb and honest story-telling, the central form of the book, creates a rich medium allowing the reader to 'recover from their own Rogue Wave experience and turn to the future.' Through the Rogue Wave archetype, Martha and Harry move deeply into the psychology, mentality, ethics, morality, and attributes of leaders in crises. As a leader and coach to leaders, I found their reflections and insights thought provoking, insightful and, most of all, helpful."

—Anne Kemp
President
Berkeley Developmental Resources, Canada

"A real world guide to navigating a crisis! A must read for a fast-moving and volatile world."

—John Kim
President
New York Life

"Hutson and Johnson 'name the beast,' helping us describe what true leaders all feel, and thereby giving us a measure more comfort facing it. The world may indeed seem more and more complex, but their work here makes our understanding of its complexity more complete. If you're the steward of a team's trust wrestling with a wicked problem, this is valuable advice—and reassurance—that you need to hear."

—Alexander Knapp
Director
AKCGlobal

"*Navigating an Organizational Crisis* is highly experiential, not theoretical. It uses stories of leaders' responses to sudden, spontaneous, and significant events to illuminate leadership resources that create growth from the peaks and the valleys in our organizational and personal journeys."

—Frank R. Lloyd, PhD
Associate Dean
SMU Cox School of Business

"A wonderful read filled with insight, metaphor and humor all embedded in the harrowing journeys of leaders who have encountered the unthinkable and found their way through. Hutson and Johnson have provided a gift here, showing us the power of story to reveal our inner wisdom, guide others through times of challenge, and ultimately renew our sense of self when it has been shaken to the core."

—Lani Peterson, Psy.D.
Psychologies and Professional Storyteller

"Effectiveness in a crisis requires agility, flexibility, and resilience, but as Johnson and Hutson clearly show, there are specific tools and strategies leaders can use to win the day. And in a crisis, it is often about winning the day, and the next day, and the one after that. They have written the Scout's Handbook for leadership in a crisis."

—Josh Sawislak
Global Director of Resilience
AECOM

"In today's business climate navigating rogue waves is the new normal. Agility and rapid course corrections with a firm, confident hand on the tiller are today's leadership requirements."

—Dean A. Scarborough
Chairman & CEO
Avery Dennison Corporation

"This book is not about common management issues. Instead it provides important insights into how leaders can cope when facing overwhelming, potentially fatal disasters. It is enriched by a super-abundance of 'you are there' case vignettes and bibliographic references. Its lessons for leaders are fresh and straightforward."

—Robert H. Schaffer
Senior Partner
Schaffer Consulting

"If you are a leader or aspire to become a leader, you must read this book. Harry Hutson and Martha Johnson have captured the essence of leadership during and after a crisis. In my opinion, their wisdom should be applied by all people, all of the time."

—Deborah Lipman Slobodnik
Principal
Options for Change, LLC

"Leadership is not just about charisma or strategic thinking; it is ultimately about perseverance and ability to lead with a human touch. Hutson and Johnson capture this notion through real stories and invite us to bring more of ourselves to the job of leadership."

—Raj Sharma
CEO, Censeo Consulting Group

"This is a boldly written book telling powerful stories of leaders meeting a 'rogue wave.' With a strong voice and well-chosen examples, it challenges readers to think about what personal qualities enable good responses to and recovery from an unplanned and unexpectedly high magnitude event. Don't think one won't come your way; it might. So, gain insights into managing one from this book."

—Naomi Stanford
Organization design consultant and author

"Hutson and Johnson face down rogue waves or the most difficult leadership crises that we can neither anticipate nor prevent. The authors show us how to use emergencies to strive, seek, endure, and thrive. This book builds your personal strength and renews the life of your organization, community, and nation."

—David Lee Townsend
Senior Adviser for Seminars
Aspen Institute

"In this volume, Hutson and Johnson offer an excellent resource for leaders facing unexpected and unpredictable crises. They synthesize knowledge from the fields of human resources, organizational effectiveness, emergency preparedness, and leadership development. And, importantly, they bring the real-life insights and experiences of thoughtful people to bear on the question: How does one lead in a time of crisis?"

—D. Susan Wisely
Scholar in Residence, MDC, Durham, North Carolina
Director of Evaluation, retired, Lilly Endowment, Indianapolis, Indiana

Navigating an
Organizational Crisis

Navigating an Organizational Crisis

When Leadership Matters Most

Harry Hutson and Martha Johnson

 PRAEGER™

An Imprint of ABC-CLIO, LLC

Santa Barbara, California • Denver, Colorado

Library of Congress Cataloging-in-Publication Data

Hutson, Harry, author.
   Navigating an organizational crisis : when leadership matters most / Harry Hutson and Martha Johnson.
      pages cm
   Includes bibliographical references and index.
   ISBN 978–1–4408–4026–5 (hard copy : alk. paper) — ISBN 978–1–4408–4027–2 (ebook) 1. Crisis management. 2. Leadership. 3. Management. 4. Organizational behavior. I. Johnson, Martha N., author. II. Title.
   HD49.H87   2016
   658.4′092—dc23   2015030799

ISBN: 978–1–4408–4026–5
EISBN: 978–1–4408–4027–2

20 19 18 17 16   1 2 3 4 5

This book is also available on the World Wide Web as an eBook.
Visit www.abc-clio.com for details.

Praeger
An Imprint of ABC-CLIO, LLC

ABC-CLIO, LLC
130 Cremona Drive, P.O. Box 1911
Santa Barbara, California 93116-1911

This book is printed on acid-free paper ∞

Manufactured in the United States of America

This book is dedicated
by Harry to his mother, Betty,
and
by Martha to her husband, Steve.

With thanks to the leaders we interviewed who opened our hearts
and minds to the challenges they face in crises.

Contents

Introduction

Service to others is the rent you pay for your room here on earth.[1]

—Muhammad Ali

What if we told you that leaders are *never* prepared for what can happen on their watch? What if we said that *crisis* is necessary for growth? And what if we explained that *service to others* is a form of *service to you*?

We are awash in a world of crises. Since September 11, 2001, public consciousness about the threat of disaster has been greatly enlarged. We have increased the priority we place on preparedness, readiness, and response, and focused great energy on understanding threats and reducing risks. In parallel, demands for more effective leadership have come from all corners, and experts and practitioners have responded with all manner of useful suggestions. Recently, and significantly, the two worlds of crisis management and leadership development have begun to overlap. Crisis management is expanding well beyond detection and rapid response to include consideration of the impact of events on decision makers. Leadership development is expanding well beyond strategic thinking, team building, and communications to include psychological and spiritual dimensions for anyone with special responsibilities functioning under pressure. However nascent, these are timely and significant studies, and we write this book to continue that work.

Our contribution is twofold. First, we have been fortunate to talk to dozens of leaders about crisis situations, and we have found enormous value in listening closely to what they describe and reveal. Theirs are not abstract, strategic, or even conceptual descriptions. They have seen the devastation of loss and death, tasted the smoke in the air, and quivered inside as they have stood in front of the microphones. Their world is real and very complicated, and it lends urgency to the topic. Their voice is the heart of our book. We have chosen to accept the truth of their experience and lean in their direction as we make connections and interpretations.

Second, we have discovered an unruly collection of common, persistent questions and extraordinary insights coming from those leaders. We set about in this book to capture and, as well as we might, frame them. We believe our role is to reveal issues and launch awareness. Some of the questions, for example, are highly resonant within the context of our culture and our fraught and volatile times:

- *Transparency:* How much truth telling should I really do?
- *Strategy:* We cannot recover the past. Where do we go from here?
- *Heroics:* How can I take care of everyone?
- *Sense making:* How do I explain what just happened?
- *Recovery:* Does resilience training work? Really?

Other little splinters of insights were much more personal, about their own needs, judgment, and resources:

- Am I a fraud? (I feel like one.)
- Why does it seem so wrong for leaders to pay attention to their own needs?
- How is it that some people show up and others disappear? Whom can I trust?
- In crisis, there is trauma. How do I handle emotional issues?

We are only scratching the surface. The outpouring in the interviews has stepped up our hope that we will entice others into this important conversation. An early reader of the manuscript commented that it is less about landing an airplane and more about getting planes to fly. We believe the questions at hand about leaders and crisis are too critical to answer glibly or to box into tight models. This is a time for opening up the thinking and the dialogue. Clearly, the leaders with whom we spoke are eager to talk and listen.

Our Story

We, Harry and Martha, met in 1979, at Cummins Engine Company, in southern Indiana. Newly released from graduate studies, we were determined to put our learning to work. We were American versions of salary men, members of an army of professionals going to the office every morning and disappearing inside the maw of the corporation. Neither of us is, at heart, a conformist, and yet it was exciting. Nothing about our experience at the motor works turned out to be regimented or faceless. Cummins was a mighty corporation but also a special place of shiny new ideas, all the more incredible because the company was located squarely in the rust belt.

It is not overstatement when we say that work was wondrous. We were both initially employed in Personnel (as it was known in those days). Harry did management development. Martha recruited talent and then moved into line management in the factory. We relished working together and with the many other young professionals who were looking for (corporate) adventure.

We were witnessing a special moment in American manufacturing, a period of hugely disruptive international competition and nearly counter-intuitive approaches to quality and processes. In time, Cummins's management stared down the crisis of foreign competition and we were lucky to have played a part in this process. Martha was on the Plant Operating Team that transformed the Cummins's ten-liter-engine assembly line with a Just-in-Time and Total Quality Management implementation. The effort was novel in those days, and few outside Japan knew if such methods would work. Harry was at the corporate headquarters where executive dynamics reflected the turmoil on the engine lines. We look back on that now and stand taller for having been part of something real and, as it happens, transformational for both organization and industry.

Martha left Cummins to weave a career on the East Coast, where she would scoot up the operating management track. Harry stayed a little longer and moved up the human resources ladder and then moved to other major organizations. We stayed in touch as much as possible given different geographies and the complexities of family, health, and calendar.

With time and a pot of coffee or over some beers, either one of us could share stories of our subsequent experiences *in* crises, as well as *with* and *as* leaders. Harry had some particularly stressful years within a global education company. Family needs were in competition with his travel schedule. It felt to him as if crises at home and work followed some insidious synchronicity. Harry was not alone in trying to get work-life balance right.

But he also had a habit of signing on with companies that were riding directly into dust storms. As the human resources person, he was front and center with the frayed behaviors that ensued. Harry works hard at getting people to see when they are their own worst enemies, and when it comes to leaders, this matters to the entire organization. Leaders' behaviors, both good and bad, are magnified in crisis.

Martha coped with two separate bosses who were bullies. In both cases she quickly removed herself from the setting, glad to get out. Yet each situation taught her something indispensable. She realized firsthand how quickly leaders lose stature when they throw around their weight. The work of a leader is a sacred calling in many ways, and when that is abused, it is not a minor slip or an excusable mistake. And that is in normal times. Imagine how significant it is for leaders to hold faith with the organization when there is a crisis.

Authenticity, adult behavior, and good communications really, really matter. Leaders are in a covenant with their followers that is much more than a technical or contractual relationship.

We can both look back on our careers now and recognize repeated patterns. Disruption was a common theme. As we lurched along, looking forward and seldom backward, we never fully grasped that climbing through one challenge or crisis did not yield victory. Nor did it yield a breathing place. We were simply next up for the next thing to happen.

For example, in the middle of the onset of international competition in manufacturing, the entire economy was gasping from strangling interest rates, adding pressure on all our workplaces. Martha struggled with the terrible surge in liability costs while at a Boston architecture firm in the late 1980s, only to slam into the demise of the Massachusetts Miracle and the collapse in real estate markets. Harry was working to bring an IPO home, while day trading on the side, when the dot-com bubble burst and he lost on both fronts. Then he set up shop as an independent contractor, which was wholly new for him and subjected him to the trials and tribulations of a new boss (himself). Later he rode the ups and downs of the oil and gas industry in Oklahoma. Martha coped with a complete restructuring of her federal agency when Congress changed its enabling legislation. In her next job, the government was restructuring after September 11, and she was in the midst of the scramble to create the new Department of Homeland Security.

Throughout our careers, we jumped from the pan into the fire and back again. And in the foreground there was the tramp, tramp, tramp of technology change, which routinely challenged and upended everyone's basic business models. Crises repeated and then recycled.

Then, some thirty years out of Cummins, Martha's career blew up. She was President Obama's Administrator of the General Services

Administration when irregularities in contracting at a training conference in Las Vegas became the scandal du jour in Washington. Martha was excoriated in front of Congress, ridiculed on the political comedy shows, and within days was at home without a job, staring at the dust on her living room furniture.

Harry called. He wanted to extend his sympathies, vent his frustrations about current-day politics, and was curious about what Martha's experience meant for her and other leaders. It was good to be back in closer touch, and we began to talk regularly.

Over the next two years, Martha worked on knitting herself and her career back together. Harry coached a bit from afar. She began to reclaim her voice and confidence by publishing a novel, *In Our Midst*, set in a small town in southern Indiana. She then devoted her time to telling her professional story in a book, *On My Watch: Leadership, Innovation and Personal Resilience*. Harry was an important guide, particularly as she wrote the final section on personal resilience. Our talks continued and lengthened.

As Martha worked through what crisis—this particular crisis—meant for her, Harry was asking what crisis meant for others. He began interviewing leaders to learn their stories. At first, he was startled by how *immediate* crisis events seemed to be for leaders, no matter how distant in the past. They told their organizational disaster stories as if they occurred yesterday, just one click behind their polite and confident exteriors. No one needed a calendar to puzzle together the details of the events. It also struck him how engaged and self-reflective people became in these conversations. Something serious had happened to them *as leaders*. Organizational crisis had intensified their awareness, shifted their assumptions about themselves, and uncovered deeper questions. It concentrated and crystallized leadership lessons.

One lesson stood out above all others: Leaders are people and can be their best only when they are pulling from their fully human selves. Crisis demands much from a leader but not necessarily from one's known bank account of skills and competences. It is a humbling thing to be, in a very public way, in charge but unable to be in control, and when logistic, operational, and reactive muscles cannot pull the weight.

Rogue Waves, an image we borrow to name massive organizational crises, are overwhelming, and they invite us to visit deeper parts of ourselves, areas not always available to us. They stir up questions of destiny and fate, and what it means to be human. The leader is the captain, and the ship is full of souls—that is the dynamic we call up and explore.

The Book

With all this grist for our mental mills, we decided to write a book together, much to the amusement (and support) of our respective spouses.

We explored what researchers and counselors had to say about leadership and crises, and we interviewed many more leaders. We were curious about what many diverse yet connected fields would have to say: neuroscience, leadership and management, storytelling, emergency preparedness and response, organizational effectiveness, and more. We talked with small business owners, Wall Street financiers, religious leaders, police chiefs, corporate executives, nonprofit heads, and many others.

Our interviews drove our project. Every story had intensity and many were similar in terms of shock, chaos, and organizational muddle. But it would be a far overreach to leap from leaders' understanding and responses to a comprehensive theory. We found some revelations, and we found some patterns. But most of all we found the infinite ingenuity of the human spirit at work.

The crucible of organizational disaster called up deeply held truths, surprising courage and discipline, and sharp awareness of the intersection of pain and life—but no checklist of skills and no preparatory curriculum. As we heard it, rather than relying on being excellent technocrats, leaders in crisis depended on being excellent human beings.

Our working title was *The Upside of Upheaval*. Exhausted by unceasing doom and gloom in the daily news, we figured that leaders needed a boost. We decided not to go there, however. We did not want to be another voice of irrational exuberance. It is bad enough that we live in a world in which ego, self-promotion, and corporate arrogance abound. It felt too boosterish for us to tout prescriptions and suggest that you, too, can find good in the bad.

Martha found it depressing when people told her she would bounce back just fine from her career stumble. She felt as if her career were being scored in some way, like the graph of her progress on her Fitbit goals. So we opted for conversations and new ideas rather than formulas and how-tos, adjusting our approach.

Harry's son, Matthew, is a science writer and he resonated with our excitement. Because he had recently interviewed fishermen for his book, *The 7 Laws of Magical Thinking*, it occurred to him we might call crises "rogue waves." This captured our imaginations because it gave us a different voice, suggesting an iconic ship captain facing terrifying dangers at sea. It speaks to the leadership-in-crisis story with great resonance. The phrase is rich in nautical imagery, and we saw value in employing a powerful word-picture to unlock habits of mind.

The subject of how leaders work in crisis seems front and center for us as Americans and as world citizens. We face significant upheavals in the economy, in technology, and in our evolving social norms. Yet we have long insisted that we can do anything, an attitude that sees disasters as something we must pounce upon and fix. How can our leaders acknowledge the gravity of circumstance in which we live and still find broader responses? Can we stay true to the spirit of progress and possibility from the heart of struggle rather than in spite of it?

Who will be interested in this book? We, the authors, represent a number of perspectives and subcultures, but we concluded at the outset we are not in search of a niche audience. We invite those who see the world as complex and leaders grounded in that reality to be readers. We may have had card-carrying reflective practitioners in our mind's eye from word one.

We retell stories from leaders, and we wrap them around interesting findings from researchers as well as thoughtful observations made by people from whom we have learned.

Chapter One: "Rogue Wave: When Catastrophe Calls"

We begin with a story about a real, Alaskan rogue wave from which we can draw many of our inferences, symbols, and ideas. We are quick to point out that despite the drama of the story, crisis is common. While we live in a world that is focused on crisis *prevention*, there is no stepping away from the reality that we are never fully in control. A Rogue Wave *will be* rolling our way, and we take a moment to lay out what that is like from behind a captain's wheel.

Chapter Two: "Hell's Bells and Buckets of Blood! Name It and Face It"

Drenched by the wave, coughing from the toxic cloud, or seeing the bomb blast real time on television does not always bring the message home. Crisis can be so disorienting that leaders may clutch. And that will not help. Responding immediately might not be easy, but leaders must name it and face it. Active response to crisis is, deep down, inherent to our character and survival instinct, and it is the first signal that the leader is leading.

Chapter Three: "The Dark Night of the Soul: When Leaders Help Themselves"

Leaders are people who, despite the demands on them by their *roles*, are not immune to in the horror and terror of the crisis. *Resilience* can be cultivated, beginning with leaders explicitly caring for themselves. They do no one any good if they pass out for lack of oxygen. *Pre-resilience*, our term, figures in that realm of capability that is already in us as human beings, the deep well of human creativity and spirit available if we can access it and trust it.

Chapter Four: "Don't Just Do Something. Be There! (For the Organization)"

In the urgency of the moment, leaders are simultaneously faced with spiritual and emotional needs of people. People need something from their leaders that is much more than action and information. They need what we call *Helpful Help*. To offer comfort, connectivity, and reassurance is not the hero's usual reaction during calamity, but when it is delivered, it is like water in the desert, and the leader is rejuvenated too. Hope allows the community to restore and renew.

Chapter Five: "It Was a Dark and Stormy Night: Leadership Storytelling"

When a real wave engulfs a lighthouse, the world's coordinates are lost. In a Rogue Wave, people want more than another weather report, they want a story that makes sense of things and provides an emotional lift. Storytelling, when practiced by a leader, may be a saving grace to bring people together, reclaim community, and reestablish direction. We see them as Storytellers-in-Chief who step up in a new and ancient way.

Chapter Six: "Whitecaps on Canal Street: A True Story of Crisis Leadership"

Rod West's story about restoring power (gas and electricity) to New Orleans after Hurricane Katrina is told in full. We push and prod ideas from previous chapters and see how they apply in practice. In the calamity of the Rogue Wave, Rod had to face the truth of the chaos, name it for others, reflect deeply to find steadying memories and messages, offer spiritual and emotional support to his associates, and communicate the truth to stakeholders and communities.

Chapter Seven: "The Calm after the Storm: Trauma, Growth, and Renewal"

Curious minds want to hear how our intrepid rogue wave sailors made out once back on land. They may also want to know if there is a pattern to all the stories they were told—especially those narratives that suggest renewal is possible after a crisis. We sketch the path of a pattern we discovered, and then we dive deeply into the issue of trauma, posttraumatic growth, and what we call Rogue Wave Renewal.

SOS is the international distress signal in Morse code—it is a signal, not an abbreviation, and so we can think of it in three ways: "Save Our Ship," or "Save Our Souls," or "Send Out Succor." Organization, people, help. That is when leadership matters most.

1

Rogue Wave: When Catastrophe Calls

Never dream with thy hand on the helm!

—Herman Melville, *Moby-Dick*

This is your first week on the job as a leader and the pace is quick, the situation is sober. You are now responsible for significant and varied assets, some human. You have already been briefed on matters related to safety and security. You have been given a list of emergency numbers, if not a red mobile phone. You are scheduled to review plans for organizational preparedness, response, and continuity for a number of possible pickles and predicaments. Truth be told, you're eager to make a real impact, and you welcome all of this information. You understand that crisis management is an essential set of executive responsibilities.

You might even relish the opportunity, should it arrive, to prove your mettle when it counts most. You have the self-assurance and confidence to believe you can handle whatever comes your way. This is good. Leaders in big roles who lack nerve are not likely to gain sea legs or spines when their boats start to sink.

The problem with this picture is the gap between your resoluteness and the reality of what we are about to describe. Some crises are roguish, and they play by their own rules. They give form to the life-isn't-fair advice we give children when the world doesn't meet their demands. Our intent is to dampen your enthusiasm for heroic leadership in the face of long odds.

Imagine a rogue wave smashing you and your organization.

Routinely, we soften and round the sharp edges of these scenarios. We imagine that when a crisis arrives, it will be little more than a new layer of complexity added to a familiar problem. It might have some new fireworks, but we think it will reside within our expectations and plans. Reasonable preparedness should suffice. We understand that prediction is an imperfect art, but we think statistically and consider that the odds are stacked against something unimaginable happening. Our technical words reassure us: probabilistic risk assessment, business continuity planning, organizational agility, and root cause analysis. We affirm the value of wariness (never paranoia) and emergency plans.

And we think we are wise to the fact that we will never be able to do enough, in advance, to ward off or be ready for the unforeseen. Crisis experts tell us to accept the fact that "perfect prevention is perfectly unattainable,"[1] and we blithely agree.

We know these things. At least we say we do. But are we whistling in the dark? Aren't we rationalizing catastrophe? What about a rogue wave—terrible to behold, impossible to manage, indiscriminate in its effects? How will you grasp apocalypse? How will *you* lead?

Some crises completely bypass what Steven Fink calls the "prodromal crisis stage,"[2] where there is a forerunner, some sort of warning. Experienced sailors know all too well about sudden squalls in the microclimates that happen under the radar and big data of weather services. Experienced captains put sudden, large waves at, or near the top of, the list of fearsome things. Taking a page from their pilot books, we extend the term "rogue wave" to mean unpredicted crises that really put leaders to the test. We believe there is great efficacy in the image, well worth our exploring together.

The field of crisis management continues to develop and offer new tools and solutions. The *Encyclopedia of Crisis Management* includes 385 signed entries by experts offering guidance for handling crises at every stage.[3] The scholars Erica James and Lynn Wooten, who are convinced that "crises are about people, and leading an organization before, during and after a crisis requires continuous focus on the well-being of those individuals," review recent research from many fields in their book, *Leading Under Pressure.*[4]

Our work builds on books such as these, joining evidence from many fields with stories we were told in interviews with leaders. We believe our insights are given force by the rogue wave form. Our thinking, however, doesn't hinge on extreme and anomalous examples. The kinds of crises we investigate are actually not as rare or exotic as we would like to believe. They pose hard questions that can sharpen and deepen leaders.

From Myth to Marine Science

A rogue wave is a dark force for sailors. Unlike a tsunami that can be traced to a geological event (and may be preceded by warnings, however brief), a rogue wave comes out of nowhere. It carries a threat of senseless malevolence.

Rogue waves can be dangerous in the extreme. They've been blamed for nearly drowning Sir Ernest Shackleton in 1916 in the Southern Ocean, sinking the SS *Edmund Fitzgerald* in Lake Superior in 1975, and almost capsizing RMS *Queen Elizabeth II* in 1995. The master of *QEII* said that the wave even in the night "looked like the White Cliffs of Dover." How often, when ships go "missing, fate unknown," could a rogue wave have been to blame?

When we give talks about crisis leadership, the seafaring sailors in the audience want to share their stories of near-escapes from harrowing events. Sometimes they're still shaken. For crews who have escaped them, large waves continue to evoke nightmares.

Stories of watery graves and heavy seas have induced chills and thrills since Noah. Through our interviews with leaders, we've learned how powerful a tale of a giant wave can be. There is great underlying energy in the image itself and so we have adopted it to focus the attention of leaders and to lay bare their essential tasks. We envisage a rogue wave as containing deep meaning and power as an *archetype*, an innate and universal pattern that can shed light on leadership under conditions of extreme threat. We call the archetype a Rogue Wave.

One of the most famous, recognizable, and frequently reproduced of all artistic images is *The Great Wave* by the Japanese woodblock artist Katsushika Hokusai, created in the 1830s. It has inspired painters, musicians, and poets and has become commonplace in marketing campaigns. The print shows fishermen in mortal danger of being dwarfed by a giant wave as they row across Tokyo Bay. Perhaps 100 impressions of the work are known to exist, and the highest quality versions are owned by major museums. Art historians theorize about why the image commands such universal interest, and why it has gone viral.[5] Our guess is that it conjures the powerful archetype, the Rogue Wave.

In order to appreciate this archetypal image, a side step is required. It is essential to grasp its nautical source and setting. We want to avoid making the image out to mean something it does not. We need to learn from the image and not tell it what we want it to mean.

To learn more about the actual, natural phenomenon called a rogue wave, we asked Dr. Charles Linwood Vincent, research professor of

Applied Marine Physics at the University of Miami, to give us a short course on the real thing:

> *A rogue wave is a term that came out of descriptions of situations that mariners kept running into. They would be out to sea in what I would consider to be typical large waves, and seemingly out of nowhere a really big wave would happen that caused them trouble or frightened them. The term "rogue" arose to suggest that the wave was not behaving the way the rest of the waves usually do. There are a couple of things to recognize. First, how frightened you are is a function of both the size of the wave and the size of your ship, so we think of rogue waves as being 20–30 m high, but if you are in a small ship, a wave 10 m high might be a rogue one to you. Second, they are relatively rare, otherwise they would not seem abnormal.*
>
> *I don't think there is any definitive consensus about their formation. The problem is that to truly validate a theory you would have to have very detailed measurements in rogue waves; we don't have that with traditional instruments, most of which measure the waves at one point over time. I think most experiences with rogue waves suggest that they have a very limited temporal and spatial extent. So you have to be very lucky or unlucky to be where one is when it happens.*
>
> *I think people commonly say a wave that is twice the significant height is rogue—no real science behind it other than such a wave would typically be rare; but it is based on a theory that is really only applicable for not very steep waves, which is not the case for storm situations. New technologies where the waves are measured with high-resolution lidars show that in steeper waves, the wave height distribution is different (from the one normally assumed) and that there are more high waves than you would have expected.*
>
> *Fronts, currents, bathymetry, or wind could locally make the waves steep so that a rogue wave can develop. It is hard to make useful predictions; also again, rogue is in the mind of the beholder and the size ship you are sailing in. Clearly large ships have been heavily damaged in really big wave events or even put them in a situation where they could not recover.*[6]

According to Professor Vincent, the essence of rogue waves is that they are not well understood; though "relatively rare," they may be a more likely occurrence than we have imagined, and they are definitely not benign. The Office of Naval Research has not yet devised a way to give navigators more than a few minutes' warning or to help them avoid routes likely to have rogue waves. All in all, it is a formidable phenomenon.

With nautical reality as a reference, we suggest that *a Rogue Wave is an archetype for a sudden, spontaneous, and significant crisis for leadership.*

A Rogue Wave event is an emergency that requires an immediate response from a leader. It is roguish because of three specific attributes:

- *Sudden* (out of the blue, fast acting, unexpected, unpredictable)
- *Spontaneous* (having multiple causes, perhaps self-generated, completely uncontrollable)
- *Significant* (consequential, implying life or death, yielding momentous success or failure)

Thanks to Professor Vincent, there is another angle that can inform us. At the intersection of oceanography and psychology, *perception* of the event is decisive. "A rogue wave is in the mind of the beholder." We impute that the power of a rogue wave story derives not only from molecules but also from the human spirit.

The rogue wave image has power and form, yet in order for it to be useful to leaders, it needs to be at the top of mind. Be clear that emergencies are part of your job and forget about trying to anticipate or prevent every bad thing from happening. Accept the likelihood that organizational crises will occur on your watch.

To bring matters home, we have a deep sea tale to tell. What follows is the story of a captain and a wave. Kale Garcia, a professional deep-sea crab fisherman in Alaska, faced a real rogue wave. Kale's story evokes basic aspects of organizational crises and the inherent responsibilities of leaders.

Captain Kale Garcia's Story

Harry interviewed Kale Garcia with his wife, Angie, and their family by phone as they sat around a table at their home in Bend, Oregon, on a sunny day in December.[7] Kale is a deep-sea crab fisherman and captain of the *Auriga*, a 167-foot trawler. The tone of the conversation was light and easy. He's told his story many times over the years. Kale sounded knowledgeable, matter-of-fact, and friendly. Given his experience and credibility, as well as the amazement factor in his tale, we were taken with his humility.

On an unusually calm and clear February night in the Aleutians over a dozen years ago, Kale and crew were traveling from King Cove, where they had just dropped off their haul, to Dutch Harbor, where they needed to resupply. On board were Angie and seven other sailors. The moon and stars were shining while Kale and Angie relaxed in the wheelhouse enjoying the quiet. Angie was sitting on the console, with Kale at the controls. There was a light breeze and a two-foot chop, so tranquil that they recall noticing a glass sitting safely on the counter. The *Auriga* was heading through the protected side of Baby Pass. Six vapor sodium lights fixed to the mast illuminated the way.

Kale was talking on the radio with his friend, Bill, as they approached a narrow stretch in the pass, a half-mile off the rocks. As they talked, something caught Kale's eye on the radar that looked like electronic clutter. He looked up and blurted, "What is *that*?"

Kale told us, "It looked like we were just going to run into a wall." He continued:

When this thing came closer, I sat down and looked up but could not see its top. It just looked like we were running into a vertical mountain. We had no idea how big it was. We were probably 30' off the water and it was more than twice our height. It was big enough to do quite a bit of damage.

What happened next sounded like an explosion, like a cannon shot, followed by blood-curdling screaming. So, of course, I thought the worst had happened. When we ran into this thing, it ripped open the front of the wheelhouse and peeled it back like a can opener. Sheets of steel were curled at the ends.

The engineer's room was right below where I was standing in the wheelhouse, and that was what the screams were about. The wave went into his room in a fraction of a second. There were big ice chunks flowing into the boat, and he got flushed out of his room, down the stairs to the galley level. But the heaters were 230 volt, so when the water contacted the heaters all the water was electrified. The first mate came running out, heard the cannon shot and the engineer screaming, stepped into the water and was also electrocuted, but he ended up falling backwards down the stairs. So now everyone is washed down the stairs except for Angie and me. You could look down the stairs and all you saw was a raging river with chunks of ice heading down into the inside of the boat.

When the wave hit the boat, it severed the air and hydraulic lines for the steering and engine controls. My first thought was that we were very close to the island, and I wanted to get through the pass and away from the rocks. I (took) four guys down to the engine room, and as we were going, the water was flowing down the alleyway on the floor and in the wires and everything was blinking and going dark. I put two guys on the throttle and two guys on the gearbox to hold it in gear. We would communicate with the radio to be able to steer boat: One would slow down and the other speed up to do transitional torque with two engines.

I ran back up to the wheelhouse after I had those guys putting it in gear, and here's Angie sitting up on the console. The lights up on the mast were still there, but the lifeboats on top of the wheelhouse had been dislodged. Both of our rafts were floating in front of us going away from the boat. Angie was saying, "Oh, look, life rafts. That's perfect, we might need some right about now," followed by the second thought: "Oh, those are our life rafts!" So now we had no life rafts. The only thing we could to do at this point was beach the boat if it came to that.

We were a half-mile off Baby Island and that's what I was concerned about; we could get set down on those rocks pretty quickly. There was a lot of current in that pass. While those guys were running the engine, I grabbed everybody else and we took the mattresses off the bunks out to the bow and chained them over this big opening. We also pumped water out of the ballast tanks. It was enough to take the hectic, crazy scene of ice and water and wind coming through that hole to where we could get on with business and figure out what we were going to do.

Dutch Harbor was about six hours away. We called ahead because we didn't know how bad it would be. Lots of water was coming into the boat. Lots of breakers had shorted out. Lots of flashlights were being used. We were just trying to nurse our way around the corner. All this happened within the space of ten minutes.

That's the rogue wave story. The thing that probably saved us was the vertical bulkhead that ran fore and aft next to the engineer's room and it was pushed back like an accordion. It was a very powerful event.

Angie continued the narrative:

There was just this one wave that hit directly on from the front. If it had hit on the side, I could imagine we could have rolled over. Most times you hear of windows blowing out. I was sitting right in front of them, and it could have been really ugly had it hit there.

Kale again:

If it hit there, she wouldn't be with us today [pause].

There was no time to turn the boat. There were only about two to three seconds from when we saw it until it mowed through us. There was only one way to go. We couldn't turn around, that would have been a bad choice. We couldn't go port or starboard. The only thing we could do is try to get through this pass to where we could get into some open water. Any other way was just too risky without engine controls. My whole purpose was to try and get us away from shore to get us some breathing room.

Kale's story includes crisis and consequence; a sequence of emergency, response, and recover; a leader performing under pressure; a situation momentarily out of control. If the wave had hit the side of the *Auriga*, she might well have capsized or crashed on the rocks. If the wave had smashed the windows in the wheelhouse where Angie was sitting, the ending could have been tragic. Under these conditions, leadership is essential, even though it may not be sufficient.

Before continuing with his story, let's explore the archetype.

The Rogue Wave Is Sudden

Kale had seconds to react and minutes to save the day. Such suddenness is malevolent. We are at the mercy of our animal instincts when we get shaken, and our rational brains do not like it one bit. "Wait, what was that? Did that really happen? Do I believe my own eyes?" No wonder the first words we want to hear from family, friends, or colleagues after a worrisome event are, "Don't worry. I'm OK." No wonder leaders in all walks of life intone the doctrine of no surprises to their staffs. We want to be warned. We want to be in front of things. When we aren't, we are rocked. Rogue Wave suddenness induces shock.

Gladden Schrock, an Atlantic fisherman dragging for shrimp off the coast of Maine, wrote to us about an incident in the "Hell's Hole" fishing grounds:

> *I happened to look off to the Nor'East, in the direction of the Pemaquid Point Light House and what I saw froze my blood. The seas were by now crashing up over the TOP of the lighthouse, while the wind, which had also increased throughout the morning, carried the "froth" of the breaking waves clear across the Lighthouse parking lot, 200 feet into the woods. It was a sight that simply escaped the bounds of one's cognitive bearings, of one's sense of "survivable events" in the instant offing.*[8]

An organization can be just as rocked as an individual. Just as circulatory shock constricts blood vessels, organizational shock inhibits the flow of vital information needed to deliver service, build product, or make decisions.

On September 11, 2001, we were confronted with the painful reality that shocks could happen at any time and impact the entire society. If we hadn't known it on September 10, by September 12 we knew that a few could terrorize the many, in an instant. Recently, we witnessed how the Ebola diagnosis of a single patient could paralyze an entire healthcare system, in a day. Repeatedly, we have seen the stock market fall precipitously in the opening moments of trading. Our world can change forever in the time it takes to hear a few words on a phone call.

We know these things, but we resist being cowed. We can't live our lives watching TV behind locked doors. We choose to take our chances out in the world.

Meanwhile, the next Rogue Wave is trolling our neighborhood, our industry, our clients, or our marketplace, ready to take us by surprise once again.

The Rogue Wave Is Spontaneous

We strive to predict the future, and we invest enormously to get in front of crises. Some disasters pay us no heed; a sudden, unanticipated tornado can make for a very long day. Kale didn't know about the wave's existence until he was looking up at it. His radar was of no help to him.

This degree of spontaneity really pushes our buttons. Our natural inclination is to feel personally implicated, to rack our brains for clues, or to hunt down guilty parties. Why me, Lord? What did I miss? Whom can I blame? Is this something I deserve? And on and on.

We suggest a different tack. Admonishing, puzzling, condemning, or self-scolding is a defensive routine with little bearing on outcomes in the moment. Look elsewhere for the source of the predicament at a more convenient time. Meanwhile, as a way to get through the crush of events, consider the notion of *fate*.

Fate is an outlier in the ideology of command and control. Many leaders ban it from their lexicon. Fate suggests surrender, or impotence, and like an act of God, it's exempt from insurance claims. To factor in fate would require relinquishing the expectation that the world is ultimately knowable. We resist that notion. We want a world in which virtue and blame are clear, where it is a waste of time to ponder the "unknown unknowns," and where we can indefinitely postpone hard questions about the randomness of life.

Nevertheless, Rogue Waves (and rogue waves) do happen. No person and no organization is ever completely safe. The discomforting backstory is that we aren't exempt from the fickleness of fate. Was it fate or good fortune that the *Auriga* was hit by a giant wave, but just happened to be facing it head-on? Neither Kale was at fault for the wave, nor could he take credit for the position of his boat in the pass.

Kale had responsibility for crew and boat, not the wave. He was the captain, not a superhero. A leader inherits responsibility for his or her organization, not the whole world. Kale's choice point was the moment he boarded, not when his engine room was awash and lifeboats were floating away. His job was to save the *Auriga*, not rail against the gods.

The Rogue Wave Is Significant

Rogue Waves can drown institutions, shatter communities, and flummox leaders. They can disrupt markets and influence the psyches of cultures. They can cause destruction and death. They can also be the leading edge of a sea change in consciousness.

Larry Barton, a crisis expert who has led responses to more than 3,400 incidents in the workplace, lists 44 recent organizational crises around the world, including the Union Carbide disaster in Bhopal and earthquakes in Turkey, from workplace and school violence to coal mine collapses, to show "what could happen." Computations expressed in numbers of casualties, dollars of losses, percentages of declines, or points on the Richter scale cannot fully capture this record of physical damage and human hurt.[9] Barton concludes: "[R]emember . . . it's a jungle out there."[10]

Today the "new normal" looks more like a new abnormal.

In our interviews we heard Rogue Wave stories about Hurricane Katrina, the Boston Marathon bombing, and the financial collapse of 2008–2009. We also heard stories about calamities that did not make national headlines but were, nonetheless, terrible. There was the death of a student in the care of his teachers, the collapse of a museum roof, a battle to save a respected company from a hostile takeover, and more. Each event represented the turning of a page, a hard lesson for a leader, and the end of an organizational status quo. Expectations were swamped or shattered. And, as if delivering insult to injury, Rogue Waves go well beyond doing damage to persons and property. They drown the familiar, the "taken-for-granted."

When domestic terrorists bombed the Alfred P. Murrah Federal Office Building on April 19, 1995, a Rogue Wave had hit the state of Oklahoma. As many as 169 people died, 490 were injured, and the United States would never be the same. The mission of the Oklahoma City National Memorial and Museum on the site of the bombing is: "We come here to remember those who were killed, those who survived and those changed forever."[11]

We talked with Larry Nichols, whose wife was gravely injured in the bombing. He was then the CEO of Devon Energy, one of the business anchors in town.[12] "No one in Oklahoma City had done anything wrong," he stated softly. Yet, the catastrophic effect was endured by all. "Everyone knew someone who was affected."

Now, two decades later, Larry is still tender on the subject.

There are certain parts of that story that, if I dwelled on them, would bring me to tears. I know exactly where they are, and so when I get to that part I just take a little detour. It's just too much—that really surprises me, but you do learn it's still there. Seeing all that human tragedy.

We pause for a moment to note that while Rogue Waves break known standards for upheaval and pain, they can also set new standards of performance and response. Oklahoma City in the wake of the bombing set a standard of what it means for a community to care. Citizens ran through smoke and debris *toward* the building rather than away. When more gloves were needed for rescue workers, every store in the area was emptied of its stock within hours. Blood donors were turned away because too many showed up. First responders weren't allowed to pay for their meals in restaurants. In the case of Oklahoma City, an entire community stood up to an unimaginable and heartbreaking Rogue Wave.

The Pattern of the Wave

Harry and his colleague Barbara Perry facilitate an exercise during strategic planning seminars where participants are asked to create an organizational timeline.[13] Typically, the group is asked to recall and retell key dates, significant stories, and random anecdotes, and it is best when a broad swath of stakeholders is involved. For example, there can be a school assemblage with teachers, administrators, staff members, students, parents, and board members present, or an equivalent grouping for an agency, a company, a community, or a religious congregation.

Imagine a roll of butcher paper 40' long with a horizontal timeline drawn through the center with a fat marking pen. Participants sign in by placing a hash mark on their starting date with the organization. Cohort groups (people who arrived within relatively the same period of time) collectively record events that they deem significant.

The most important part of the process is the requirement to place sticky dots above or below recorded events to characterize how positively or negatively they are perceived. Drawing lines to connect dots sequentially yields a pattern. The purpose of the activity is to depict the past, look for patterns, draw conclusions, and make plans for a new day.

Organizational timelines constructed in this manner make shared organizational experience visible to all. Participants can discuss the patterns they observe in the depiction of their shared history and construct the way forward together.

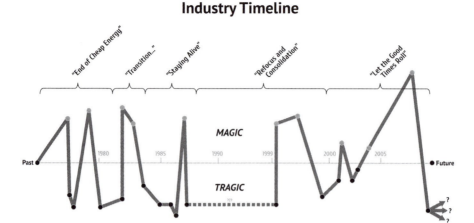

Figure 1.1

Having witnessed the creation of many organizational timelines over many years and in all sorts of settings, Barbara and Harry have noticed something distinctive about the patterns that the groups see in the dot-to-dot line they create. It is perceptible in the Industry Timeline displayed in Figure 1.1.

The shape doesn't undulate like a sine wave, nor does it conform to other rhythmic waveforms. In fact, there is usually no pattern at all. The shape is *roguish*. The timeline is consistently inconsistent. The curve is nonlinear and complex, with sudden spikes, long swoops, plateaus, and sketchy areas where there is not enough information. A pattern of randomness emerges. Reactions among members of each group are also anything but similar. They range from "ouch" to "aha, now I see."

Given how much time we spend at work and how much we are invested in organizations where we work (or study or worship), we might all welcome some steadiness, routine, and predictability. Wild occupational gyrations and disorienting organizational shifts all serve up anxiety and cause us to lose sleep. Organizational timelines reveal the unsettling picture of fluctuation and instability that often accompanies our work.

The good news is that this is a pragmatic and honest assessment, and groups that grasp that quickly do well. This revelation of randomness need not be a crushing conversation for an organization that wants to survive and thrive. While there is little that will be guaranteed, most must be earned, and little credit is granted for what happened yesterday.

Jim Henderson, who was president of Cummins Engine Company during our tenure there, the 1970s, a volatile era indeed, routinely repeated to the organization: "There is no safe harbor in our business, no matter how much we would like one." Competition, change, and the need to improve are constant.

It would be rare indeed for an organization never to experience some blow after which it must search for identity, meaning, and purpose. The Rogue Wave archetype resonates with us precisely because we all have experienced upheavals and unexpected crises in our lives. The job of a leader is to help us remember that Rogue Waves are endurable and may even be strengthening to an organization. Without stress, we do not grow; without dissonance, we do not seek; without disaster, we are not tested. The book of Genesis contains that very story. We cannot become fully human sheltered in the Garden of Eden.

The seemingly uneven waveform created in the timeline group activity corresponds to one of the deepest and most complex patterns in nature, the human heartbeat. Barry Cipra, a mathematician, reports that healthy hearts are actually "part of a large feedback system whose dynamics are nonlinear, non-stationary, and multi-scale."[14] Healthy heartbeats are neither "lub-dub" consistent nor erratically arrhythmic. Healthy heartbeats are fractal, which means they are patterns in complex physical systems that maintain "adaptive variability."[15]

While we usually think of the heart as steadily beating away with a drummer's rhythm, the healthy heart actually jumps, ebbs, and flows, synchronized with the relentless onslaught of surprising events. The heart, the organization, and the sea have natural rhythms characterized by suddenness and spontaneity. Neither can the core pulse of leadership ever be one of mechanical metronomic consistency.

For leaders, the archetype serves up several important reminders. A Rogue Wave is an unwelcome threat. You did not cause it or fail to anticipate it, but it showed up anyway. You never courted or invoked it, but now you must live with it. And there will be more events like these than you care to admit.

And it may save your bacon if you remember just this: While your core will be shaken when a Rogue Wave arrives, the real issue will not be the wave. The issue will be you. It will challenge you, as a leader, on your most fundamental assumptions about your personal leadership attributes. Can you suspend your need to feel in control? Can you deal with the real situation? Will you be able to postpone blame, excuses, analyses, distractions, surrenders, escapes, and denials? Can you be like Kale, grab a flashlight, head to the engine room, and lead?

A Rogue Wave never fits a standard shape or size, nor does it leave predictable results in its aftermath. Sometimes a short, steep disruption can have a very bad effect, and a big rolling change may ultimately prove benign. Or vice versa. To increase your chances of finding a way through, remember that the seaworthiness of the "boat" (this means you) is more germane than the character of the menace.

In the most extreme cases, you will need every bit of *you* at the helm. Whether a Rogue Wave has just rocked your boat, office, schoolroom, sanctuary, emergency room, or factory floor, you must lead. Life happens, which is why leadership matters most.

2

Hell's Bells and Buckets of Blood![1]
Name It and Face It

I can see no way out but through—

—Robert Frost[2]

The ship has hit the fan. You're the captain of the organization, and you're facing a frightening reality beyond your worst nightmare. Whatever your good fortune has been up until now, whatever your experience and hard-won skills, you are up against it. Something really bad has blown in on your watch.

There's no time to think but you can't stop thinking. And you can't think fast enough. What was that, you say? What's happening now? What options do we have? Do we batten down the hatches or head for the lifeboats? You're caught in a quick-moving hell where "nothing connects with nothing," as T. S. Eliot described Dante's Inferno. All eyes are on you. You're the leader.

Captain Garcia had two or three seconds to glance up from an ominous image on his radar screen and witness a giant wave towering above. Then BOOM, and blood-curdling screams! We know what Kale did. What would you do?

Take a lesson from the experience of the *Auriga*. When a mountain of water is bearing down, you want to face it from the bow, the strongest part of the ship. Kale said, "What saved us was the vertical bulkhead." As a metaphor for all crises, this means you confront them head-on. Take responsibility in two ways. First, name the emerging reality. Figure it out fast, say out loud what it is, and spread the word. Second, face the wave. Take command.

Kale's story illustrated these two imperatives. He made two judgments that may have saved them: Keep going, and don't abandon ship. Captain Garcia recognized and named the threat at once, and then he faced it immediately. He exhibited quick thinking and resolve. "We're not getting in that water," he told his wife.

Making sense of things and taking command play out differently in each version of a Rogue Wave, and yet, these activities are *always* the two tasks of leadership under pressure. They are the two first responses necessary to help organizations.

When leaders refuse to respond immediately to a crisis, they paralyze themselves and those around them. On the other hand, when they swing an organization into action without a concerted "call to arms," without naming the crisis, they create confusion and bewilderment. Hesitation prolongs agony; helter-skelter behavior exacerbates bedlam. When trouble is at the door, the first task of leadership is to name it and face it.

No doubt you have done some preparatory work for emergencies. You have reasonable confidence that you are ready in case something bad happens, even if you can't forecast what it might be. You haven't been a shirker; you've made plans. You have experience. You are reliable, responsible, and alert.

Planning for the future is always the best policy. It is the motto of both the Boy Scouts and the Girl Scouts—"Be Prepared!" However, we caution, your planning may get in your way.

Organizational researchers Karl Weick and Kathleen Sutcliffe claim that our plans can actually be harmful in a crisis. Plans are built to address our expectations and are limited to what we can imagine on a clear sunny day. Plans assume our responses will be the same as they were in the past. And, in response to many crises, this may be true. But when a real Rogue Wave hits, these plans for quotidian and anticipated crises may direct us to perform actions that are formulaic, automatic, and mindless.[3]

In response to a sudden event, leaders may enjoy a temporary advantage by "listening to their gut," demonstrating a decisive and cool manner. When their leadership automatic pilots are well conditioned, they judge situations quickly, and don't flinch from demanding action. There may be some advantage to this quick response step-up. For better or worse, some of these leaders may have instinctively felt the limits inherent in the plans, and they may have repeated Mike Tyson's line: "Everybody has a plan until they get punched in the mouth."[4] But even if a leader's instinct for quick action seems to be the right response in the first moments after the Rogue Wave, there is a real danger that "gut" will mislead.

Why Now?

John Kim, a senior executive at New York Life, experienced his Rogue Wave moment in September 2008, 10 days before Lehman Brothers collapsed.[5] After a call with brokers trying to do a deal, he thought, "This is going to be really bad. These guys actually don't know what's going on." John said:

> I get paid to be analytical, but I was wrong on both the duration and extent of the financial crisis. I was shaken both personally and professionally to the core, and I experienced an anxiety level as high as I've ever felt.

John managed a portfolio of assets worth a quarter of a trillion dollars. He was also responsible for the welfare of his organization and, of course, his family. He had to move quickly to address one catastrophe after another. *Now* was the order of the day.

A Rogue Wave starts the stopwatch. The clock is ticking for leaders to respond, for two important reasons.

First, the organization will begin to feel it has been somehow deceived, and suspicion of its leaders will begin to brew. Even beloved leaders need to grasp how their followers may begin to see them as betrayers. Their personal credibility is on the line. When bad things happen to good organizations, people look, by way of explanation, to the flaws they previously ignored. A process of demonization begins.

According to Ian Mitroff, founder of the University of Southern California Institute for Crisis Management, "The feelings of being betrayed by a crisis are basically the result of the feelings that the CEO and top management should have taken better care of us."[6] Mitroff lays out seven betrayals: *You* failed to make the world safe, failed to make the world fair, failed to make the world stable, failed to limit the crisis, failed to be inherently good, failed to make me good, and/or failed to warn me that you would betray me.[7]

When a crisis hits, people feel betrayed, distressed, uncertain, and scared, and they also feel they have been naïve and vulnerable to deceit. The world has turned on them and they're deeply troubled by the surprise. They become suspicious and hyperalert for signals that they've been taken for fools or rubes. They don't want to be caught again in such circumstances, and they scrutinize their leaders for any evidence of falseness. Leaders who sugarcoat, obfuscate, duck details, talk legal jargon, deliver bad news as if it were a printout, or try to pull off a public relations stunt are in deep jeopardy. Their organizations will remember the maxim: "Fool me once, shame on you. Fool me twice, shame on me!"

In the hours after the assassination of President John F. Kennedy, Lyndon Johnson acted to forestall a national sense of betrayal. Several scenarios were possible, but Johnson insisted upon following the one that he understood would convey the necessary message. By returning immediately to Washington accompanied by Mrs. Kennedy, he demonstrated leadership in the face of the world's shock and anguish. The presence of Mrs. Kennedy at his side, resisting her instinct to retreat from the media to the safety and security of family and performing one of her last public duties, was a key element in sending the message that the country was safe. She demonstrated her own sense of security with Johnson as leader, passing a symbolic mantle of leadership to him. Johnson acted with understanding of the collective need to mourn the loss of a beloved leader and to feel secure that the U.S. government would continue unabated, even in the face of confusion, disruption, and such a violent betrayal of trust.

The second reason that leaders must respond promptly is that the painful experience is already solidifying like concrete in the organization's memory. Doing or saying the wrong thing in a crisis can certainly be a problem, but doing nothing is lethal. In the words of Warren Buffett: "One's objective should be to get it right, get it quick, get it out, and get it over. You see, your problem won't improve with age."[8] Leaders can't play it safe and win. They are already one-down in the eyes of their followers because the crisis has happened. If they don't show up, and show up soon, they'll be two-down.

What if the leader had nothing to do with causing the crisis? Rogue Waves are prototypical "acts of god." Does the leader deserve the fallout, and is it fair that their careers may be in jeopardy? The truth is that *no one cares*. Leaders don't accrue much sympathy. No one RSVPs the invitation to their pity party. It is probably wise not to state the fact that "it wasn't my fault." They can figure that out for themselves.

Before the smoke has cleared, what should a leader stand up and say? The director of research at the National Preparedness Leadership Initiative, Eric McNulty, listened carefully to Thomas Frieden, head of the Center for Disease Control when Ebola cases were discovered in the United States. Frieden said confidently, "I have no doubt that we'll stop this in its tracks in the U.S." However well intended his statement,

Frieden did not understand how completely the country was both on high alert and extremely distrustful. Each word uttered by a public official was a test of her or his credibility. Frieden's comments fanned the flames of anxiety instead of reassuring or truly informing the public, and further, he was wrong. McNulty warns: Always underpromise and overdeliver.[9]

The challenge is to be right—enough—while being empathetic. This is not a simple challenge. When leaders say, "Don't worry!" they are telling people how to feel. When leaders declare, "We've got it," the subtext is, "That's all you need to know." When leaders say they are in charge of situations that we perceive to be out of control, we know we're being protected or played.

Your words matter and your implicit messages matter even more.

Timing matters, too. While the story is still unfolding, there is urgency in the need for leaders to speak truth, be real, and help to make sense of what is happening. When the early moments are wasted, collective rehabilitation is painfully prolonged; many workers may never get back to work at pre-crisis levels of productivity. "An organization can get its phone lines back up and have its computers backed up ... but its workers may still be screwed up," according to Gerald Lewis, a crisis management expert who has performed more than 500 critical incident debriefings in varied work settings.[10]

There are further potential dangers ahead for a leader. As mentioned above, a process of demonization of a leader may begin. When employees feel alienated from supervisors and the organization, they may flee toward the perceived safety of like-minded subgroups, blaming "The Man" (or "The Woman") for the Rogue Wave.

On September 12, 2001, Jeffrey Kleinberg, a therapist in New York City, was promptly back in his office meeting patients. He listened to his clients as they bemoaned the attack; for some, it "had significantly changed their view of work and the workplace."[11] They felt betrayed by their bosses and were disengaged from their jobs. They were suffering. While still going to work, for them it was as if "the lights are on, but nobody's home."

Kleinberg, having studied natural and human-made disasters all over the world, names this postcrisis reaction "worker's block." Not an illness per se, worker's block is both a personal and a corporate barricade. The indicators are absenteeism, increased conflict among employees, low morale, poor performance, and early retirement. When worker's block takes hold, work culture becomes rife with dissension, rumor, and suspicion. Authority figures are the first to be blamed. One person told

Kleinberg, "We shouldn't have trusted them before; why should we believe them now?"[12]

The reasons for worker's block are easy to fathom. Work is central to our identity, and for many of us the workplace is an island of safety, a place where we can feel focused and empowered. If our work life is unexpectedly and completely disrupted, we feel personally attacked and gravely threatened. In our weakened state we are vulnerable to all manner of misconceptions and confusions. We can't think very clearly about what any of this means.

Employees may disengage emotionally at work, perhaps reestablishing a focus upon friends and family. It then becomes harder for them to regroup with colleagues and to engage in the work of making collective sense. Or, according to Kleinberg, people become immobilized by "waiting for the next shoe to drop." As one of his patients told him, life is being lived "one nanosecond at a time."[13]

While grim, these reactions are understandable and are important for a leader to grasp. Why would workers *not* be blocked? A Rogue Wave has come out of nowhere, in an instant, and delivered a gigantic load of disorder.

Fear in an organization can compound quickly. We want to know whether it could be muted or extinguished, so it doesn't recirculate and grow. Recent research into how memory works offers clues.[14] Our memories evolve, similar to what happens in the "grapevine" game in which a message is passed from the mouth of one person to the ear of another. The message inevitably shifts and changes, becoming unrecognizable to the person who first shared it. When we access a memory repeatedly, our last recollection is often, for better or worse, an "improved" version of the original event, so we unconsciously choose it. In other words, we think the last thing we tell ourselves is our best memory.

There may be some good news in these findings. If our grapevine memory chains can be disrupted, the feelings they carry along with them can be updated. Daniela Schiller and her neuroscience colleagues at the Mt. Sinai School of Medicine have performed simple experiments to investigate this possibility. Participants are buzzed with light shocks when blue squares show up on a computer screen; measurements are taken of the sweat on their skin. After a few of these buzzes, participants become "fearful" of the blue squares. When blue squares are no longer connected to shocks, this fear response dissipates. But timing is of the essence to counteract a fear response. Nonshock blue squares must be used very soon after exposure to the original shocking blue squares in order to have the desired efficacy.[15]

Here's the lesson for leaders from that experiment. Leaders are in a time-sensitive setting for influencing collective memory. The sooner a crisis is faced and named, the sooner a positive process of reconsolidation can begin. The organization doesn't want to be fooled or betrayed again. Without swift intervention to assuage fear, people will return to their most recent, frightening memories and they will act under the influence of that fear.

Even under normal and routine conditions, speed is necessary. Jack Zenger and Joseph Folkman, founders of their eponymous consulting firm, wanted to know more about the relationship between speed and perceived leadership effectiveness.[16] They created a "speed index" that measured how quickly leaders spot trends, respond to problems, and make needed changes. They analyzed 360-degree feedback evaluations for thousands of leaders to find out how well speed correlated with evaluations of the top leaders in their pool. They found that few leaders were "good but slow" and fewer still were "fast only"—95 percent were *both effective and quick*.

Then they analyzed a pool of data from more than 700,000 reports to see what distinguished successful and speedy leaders from the rest. What was the number one factor reported?

People who work with them trust their ability to use good judgment and make effective decisions. Without trust, colleagues resist moving fast (or at all).

The Zenger and Folkman study connects speed with effectiveness and trust. *Pace*, they conclude, is an enormous factor in shaping the attitude of employees. "Let's face it—slow is often boring." In a Rogue Wave, slow is more than boring—it can be deadly.

Name It!

"If You See Something, Say Something." That's the message posted online, on billboards, and on public transportation, courtesy of the Department of Homeland Security. Implicit in this slogan is an imperative. When something happens, notice it. Point it out. Don't leave it to others. If you are there, give it voice. Don't gulp and swallow. Speak up. Sighting it means you have an obligation to cite it. *Name it*.

Speaking up and talking is crucial in a crisis. A threat can't be left howling at the door, anonymous, formless, without an attempt at description. A Rogue Wave can be disaster enough. It will be a double disaster if it robs us of our chance to fight back. Knocked flat on our backs, we might not yet be able to take a swing and deliver a punch, but we can still speak, and words are very powerful first weapons. Just as victims of crimes perpetuate their state of shock until they can name their aggressors, putting a label on an evil is a first step toward holding your own ground. When a leader takes the earliest opportunity to name the wave, it's a powerful assertion. The leader is effectively standing up and, most certainly, weighing in. Coherent and defiant, the leader's response will be noticed. Courage will be emulated.

The quandary is what to do when information is absent or conflicting. The noted sociologist Erving Goffman shines light on how impression management exacerbates the difficulty in flagging down a Rogue Wave. When trying to understand things when the facts are hidden from view, a leader must rely on substitutes for those facts: anecdotes, appearances, predilections, biases, hunches, and so on. Real causes, impacts, and consequences are not yet known, so the more a leader tries to solve mysteries unripe for solution, the more the leader must rely on impressions.[17] You must say something, but what?

Even when facts are known, naming something sudden, spontaneous, significant, and *negative* is a true test of leadership. Leaders hate to invite reaction, to create panic—or be wrong. The executive mantra that "you can't bring up a problem unless you have a solution" is itself part of the problem.

If we ignore our demons, they will bite us. We want to defang them, not sharpen their claws. We want to usurp their power over us and make them *uninteresting*. Noam Shpancer, a professor and practicing clinical psychologist, explains: "Familiar things get boring." So when we avoid things, from the unpleasant to the truly bad, we don't allow them to become familiar, expire, lose their attraction for us, or simply go away.[18] What we fear, when we try to look the other way, grows in its interest and remains, tantalizingly, out of sight.

After giving away his valuable cufflinks to a fan, Frank Sinatra is said to have remarked, "If you possess something but you can't give it away, then you don't possess it . . . it possesses you."[19] Sinatra's comment is as true for our fears and anxieties as it is for jewelry. Face up to your dread or it will face up to you.

The storyteller Lani Peterson advises that you must "walk toward the wind."[20]

Hovering in the background is a more profound force. A Rogue Wave's disruption foreshadows the dread of annihilation. People turn their heads when they see carnage, agony, or horror. What terror management psychologists call "mortality salience"—the awareness that death is inevitable—can occur on a mass scale. When members of an organization are at once made aware of life's limits, there can be an unmanageable number of reactions. Some Rogue Waves are "so complex and catastrophic," and their effects so profound and diverse, leadership can be marginalized as a force for recovery.[21] To stare into the deep abyss of decimation requires courage and a true sense of calling. Leaders must be able to reach those depths to name what is happening when people fear the worst.

Mortality salience can also exist at an organizational level, when members and associates become aware that their institution may expire. During the 2008 financial collapse and subsequent recession, nonprofit organizations were shaken along with everyone else. Steve Brigham, former president of America Speaks, recalls with personal and professional anguish how his organization tried, and failed, to ride out the crisis.[22]

America Speaks had successfully facilitated a remarkable community process after Hurricane Katrina, one that developed new working partnerships between organizations and citizenry. Facing its own Rogue Wave as funding and business dried up, the question was, Could America Speaks do something similar for itself? It was a matter of principle that the answer would be "yes." Its organizational mission was to offer a way through great, threatening problems, and to suggest new ways to overcome tough times collectively.

According to Brigham, "Our core belief is that you shouldn't be making key decisions in the aftermath without seriously and genuinely getting citizen voices in the mix." But the organization's leadership, board, and stakeholders struggled to find a way to apply their mission and deepest personal values to America Speaks itself. Meanwhile, the recession gnawed away at prospects and confounded the shared sense of what to do. Meaningful conversations among themselves aside, stark funding realities overwhelmed resolve. Time ran out, and they closed doors in 2013. Sometimes Rogue Waves sink good ships with their captains and crew aboard.

Speaking truth to the power of a Rogue Wave is harrowing. It's not easy for a leader to speak truth even to a handpicked team on a routine day. Leaders don't get much practice in straight, honest talk in normal organizational life. How can that be?

Wilfred Bion's psychoanalytic formulation of group life offers a perspective on the underpinnings of distorted communications. According to Bion, most members of "basic" groups (his term for groups *unable* to work well together) prefer to play follow-the-leader rather than take responsibility for their growth and development. They want to avoid the anxiety of learning something new. They will even follow an incompetent leader if they can evade responsibility.

When basic group members say they want to learn from experience, according to Bion, it's pretense. They really hate it. And when survival is threatened by the foolish or cowardly actions of their group, each person's individual need to feel safe and secure takes precedence over any other possible action.[23]

Bion is describing what happens when a crisis is never named. A leader who can't rise above his team's fears and phobias and won't insist on adaptation, is a failure. Such a leader is likely aspiring to "be a magician or behave like one,"[24] by pursuing security at any cost. The key concept in this case is *magic*—it's not *reality*.

Watch out for these dysfunctional leadership behaviors: downplaying internal criticism while intensifying in-group loyalties, firing away at perceived enemies (fight), and cutting losses by jumping ship (flight). This is leadership "from the middle"—mirroring the team's worst tendencies and not doing the work of finding the "direction home." Playing it safe is actually playing with fire.

Weak leaders who don't/won't/can't name disasters are problematic. Much worse is the troubled or injured organization that blindly follows this leadership.

Leaders must lead by staying rooted in *external* realities and resist being captured by the *internal* dynamics of the organization. They need to distance themselves from prevailing frights and fantasies; they need independence in thought, feeling, and deed as well as the courage to tell the truth.

To reassert the obvious point: Leadership truth-telling may be difficult, but it must be grounded and secured in verbal communication. Conscious mental activity in a work team, and in any grouping of teams that constitutes a company or community, relies upon talking and listening. Silence from leadership in a Rogue Wave evokes mortal fear. Leaders are central to organizational survival through their use of meaningful verbal messaging.

The best leaders embrace their responsibilities as truth tellers. They use history to inform and enhance the work of the present. They use the truth of "how we got here" to make clear what needs to happen next. They have a way of exorcising organizational demons, calling attention to the dead moose on the table, and coaxing the skeletons out of the closet. Previous errors can become the foundations for best practices going forward. The ghosts of the past can stop haunting current leaders if the ghosts are given due respect—they can be recreated as your venerated ancestors and knowing elders.[25]

The University of North Carolina at Chapel Hill, a complex institution that sits at the center of the state's identity and economy, is struggling with a rolling Rogue Wave at least 14 years in duration. Its athletic department is accused of finding ways to circumvent academic standards for the benefit of their teams—athletes were given special treatment and sometimes even enrolled in courses that never met as classes. UNC is not the only university to have indulged in such practices; nevertheless, the university's response has been slow and convoluted. No one has clearly and conclusively named the crisis and the omission is creating uncertainty. A campus minister told us that she gets two questions from students: "What is the purpose of the University?" And "Why aren't our elders providing models of truth-telling?"

President David Boren at the University of Oklahoma provided a stark contrast. He named a campus fraternity's shameful behavior in clear terms, without hesitation and with passion. When a video surfaced showing chapter members singing a racist chant, Boren condemned it and took immediate action. He shuttered the fraternity, saying: "I don't want [those responsible] here. I may even personally pay bus fare for them if they go somewhere else."[26] Here is his no-holds-barred online posting:

> *To those who have misused their free speech in such a reprehensible way, I have a message for you. You are disgraceful. You have violated all that we stand for. You should not have the privilege of calling yourselves "Sooners." Real Sooners are not racist. Real Sooners are not bigots. Real Sooners treat all people with respect. Real Sooners love each other and take care of each other like family members.*
>
> *Effective immediately, all ties and affiliations between this University and the local [fraternity] chapter are hereby severed. I direct that the house be closed and that members will remove their personal belongings from the house by midnight tomorrow. Those needing to make special arrangements for positions shall contact the Dean of Students.*
>
> *All of us will redouble our efforts to create the strongest sense of family and community. We vow we will be an example to the entire country of how to deal with this issue. There must be zero tolerance for racism everywhere in our nation.*
>
> *President Boren.*[27]

Boren's naming of racism as the evil on the table—in the earliest moments of this Rogue Wave—is a model of truth-telling done at the right moment. As we write, the story evolves. Robust discussions of the principle of free speech, the purpose of a university, the role of fraternities, the ongoing struggle against racism, and the responsibilities of a leader are unfolding in the aftermath of Boren's strong statement and position.

Multiple outcomes on all these complex issues are possible. What is least likely though is that the collective consciousness at OU will return to its previous status quo. Boren called out an ugly truth and disrupted mindless assumptions at his university.

Boren acted in sync with the advice of Norman Augustine, a successful former CEO: "The bottom line of my own experience with crises can be summarized in just seven words: 'Tell the truth and tell it fast.' "[28]

Speed is essential to effective truth-telling. But telling truth fast requires trust. No matter what truth is being proclaimed or how quickly the word has gotten out, willing followership requires trust in leadership.

"You can't sleep fast," it is said, nor can you build trust fast. Trust needs to be cultivated well before a crisis, nurtured through the ups and downs of routine times. Only then can it be available to fill in and around the abruptness with which a leader has to cut through the murkiness and chaos of calamity and name the resultant mess.

A recent study using field data on real executives and their immediate staffs helps us understand how leaders build trust with their followers. The researchers employed 360-degree feedback data on 266 managers in a leadership course. They correlated assessments of their leadership approach—personal leadership, contextual leadership, and relational leadership—with measures of how well they were trusted by their followers.

- *Personal leadership* means leader-specific qualities such as passion, expertise, and authenticity.
- *Contextual leadership* is sense-making: creating coherence, explaining responsibilities, and clarifying ambiguities.
- *Relational leadership* includes concern for others, respect, and fairness.

The results of the study show that all three routes lead to trust, but *relational leadership* was found to be the strongest predictor, because it is the method by which leaders bring their personal qualities to life.[29]

When leaders care about others, it makes all the difference. Followers will care *right back*—for each other, for their leaders, and for themselves. Without trust, a leader is a captain without a ship, a crisis reporter with no one listening. This is not new news, but defines the *reciprocity* that allows a leader to name something big, bad, and horrible—and be heard.

In the early days of management science, Chester Barnard put trust at the center of his thinking on how executive leadership actually works.[30]

For Barnard, trust is integral to morality, authenticity, and authority and is essential if leaders are to be followed *willingly*. Naming the crisis is the starting gunshot to begin a disaster response, not only because it gets things moving but also because it helps to build trust and enhances prospects for survival.

Try this as a thought experiment more than a practical exercise. Tailor the following template to suit your Rogue Wave and be inspired to launch from there. Imagine speaking words such as these to ensure you've named it.

> *I'm concerned about the impact of this crisis on every one of you, as well as our customers, suppliers, and everyone who counts on us for their livelihood . . . As one of your leaders, I assume full responsibility for the predicament we're now in . . . What we had anticipated and prepared for was "X" but this situation is "X plus" or even "Y." Some things have gone well . . . And some things haven't, but we're making plans now to find remedies or replacements . . . Make no mistake, with your help we'll get through this . . . This is where we're heading, and these are our immediate next steps . . . Specifically, here's what we need from you . . . We'll respond quickly on any new issues that arise . . . We fully intend to survive and thrive as a stronger, better, wiser, and more successful organization. That is our commitment to you, to us, and to everyone who depends on us.*

Having now named the Rogue Wave and broadcast the truth, leadership must face it.

Face It!

Vincent Strully is the CEO and founder of the New England Center for Children (NECC), a Massachusetts-based school for autism.[31] NECC had always been a very good school, and Vincent enjoyed his leadership role. The school was his creation, after all.

Vincent admits he had reached a point where the organization was well established and he was cruising along. The operation was successful, well structured, and orderly. Then came a Rogue Wave. In the storm's wake, Vincent changed, and so did NECC.

On a Friday afternoon, Vincent got a telephone call reporting that a popular student at his school had just died. It was later determined that the student had succumbed to a rare medical disorder, but his death occurred while NECC teachers were restraining the boy in order to limit his self-injurious behavior. The event was shocking, tragic, and, for Vincent, a "life-changing" Rogue Wave.

Vincent was self-confident and capable, and he says he "always knew he had this kind of responsibility," but this event forced him to analyze his life and "look at everything." Vincent rededicated himself to NECC. He faced the calamity, stepping in with sensitivity and intense resolve. He led the school in reexamining its care practices and putting new protocols in place designed to de-escalate behavioral crises and maintain safety while avoiding physical confrontation. The school's reputation, its growth at home and abroad, and its special standing in the world of autism are the rewards of Vincent's ferocious new passion. The jolt "plugged him into the school" in a new way.

Vincent says, "This is what I was meant to do."

Vincent's example raises two core questions for leaders: How can one turn and march right into the epicenter of an organization explosion? What makes that possible?

Imagine you're in the deepest part of the woods and, suddenly, you see a big brown bear (a grizzly?). Your immediate impulse is physical. You might freeze, but you probably would run. And if you run, here's a simple question for you: Why would you run?

The answer may surprise you, unless you are an outdoorsman. If you say you should have run from the bear because you feared being eaten, or clawed, or asphyxiated by bear smell, well, you were wrong. It's the other way around. Running from the bear *caused your fear*. Your body ran away and your fright had to catch up.

William James, philosopher, psychologist, and outdoorsman, noticed and named our bear back in 1884, but we continue to look with perplexity at what he saw. We prefer to feel we are in control. Our brains want to think of themselves as powerful and important, able to leap tall feelings in a single bound, able to direct the operations of humble feet on the ground. But our bodies have the first power of response, and we're actually much better off for it—especially if we live in the woods. Imagine having to do a lot of thinking about that bear, perhaps wondering where the bear hibernated, or if the bear is a protected species, or something else equally cognitive. It isn't going to happen that way. Instead, our bodies will take over and see that we hotfoot it down the trail while our minds are struggling to catch up.

When we are deeply surprised, we respond physically, through our bodies. The hormone and neurotransmitter, adrenaline, takes over and we make tracks—or we put up a fight. Our feelings and thoughts have to catch up. The bodily response precedes the emotional response.

Hank Paulson, Secretary of the Treasury during the financial upheaval of 2007–2009, admits he is prone to bouts of dry heaves when under pressure. According to CBS News, when Lehman Brothers, the big investment bank, was about to collapse, and Paulson, working the phones with Timothy Geithner, failed to find a buyer, he recalled: "My stomach tightened up and it was one of those times during the crisis where I was momentarily overcome by fear."[32] His body registered the disaster. In its aftermath, he moved to the next round of work to be done to rescue the financial system.

Tony Vaughn, currently an executive at Devon Energy, was instructed to sell a business he was managing to the best buyers, PDQ. He knew he "had to put the leadership hat on and go, like a fireman going into a burning building." He did an admirable job and was even applauded by the last group of departing employees.[33] Tony spent the next year realizing what he had been through, absorbing the experience, and feeling weary. His feelings needed time to catch up with his activity.

When Stephanie Streeter, then CEO of Banta Corporation, emerged from a backpacking trip in the wilds of Montana into an area of cell phone service, she received an urgent call. Her company was in play, the target of a hostile takeover bid. Taking barely a moment to explain the situation to her husband, she headed for the car, asking him to drive quickly to the airport. She stayed glued to the phone: "Just get me there," she said.[34]

We're genetically coded to throw ourselves into gear. Facing a Rogue Wave, leaders register the situation, see the danger, name the monster, and move. Only later do they fully recognize what has happened, assimilate its meaning, and adjust their feelings. This is why people panic *after* a disaster. They're catching up with themselves.

Leaders can't sidestep crisis, dive behind a door, or get it wrong when destruction looms. As the world shatters, people need to be led by leaders more than at any other time. The leader's pact with the organization is stripped to its essentials, a covenant that requires trust, truth, and *action*.

Vincent Strully, Hank Paulson, Tony Vaughn, and Stephanie Streeter had to react swiftly and sort out their feelings "on the go." These were not times to stop, look, and listen. They were, straightforwardly, times to don the leadership suits, strap on the hard hats, grab the life vests, cowboy up, and *face it*. Saying "uncle" just wasn't one of the choices.

The experience of having succeeded or survived in bad times, during traumas and tragedies, is formative. Having stared into the abyss once, a leader will be hardened and clear, better off the next time around. With experience, the role and responsibility of being a leader becomes embodied.

Embodiment is at the heart of crisis leadership and is at the soul of the ongoing role of leadership. We note that some of our favorite leader admonitions are clichés that rely on bodily actions. Take a look at this collection:

Stand tall
Carry your fair share
Put some skin in the game
Walk in the other person's shoes
Put your best foot forward
Face facts
Fail forward
Roll up your sleeves
Brace yourself
Stay on the balls of your feet
Keep your eye on the prize
Walk the talk/talk the walk
Keep your nose to the grindstone
Let your actions speak louder than your words
Lead by example
Lend a hand
Eat your own dog food
Lean in

Frank Lloyd, a leadership development executive says, "You put your watch on the other wrist."[35] Robert Townsend, author and former president of Avis Rent a Car, is often quoted as saying, "A good leader needs to have a compass in his head and a bar of steel in his heart."[36]

No doubt about it. We have a primal need for leaders to be real, present, and fully alive. The Wizard of Oz is the archetypal fraud whose powerful image was exposed as smoke and mirrors, disclosing the reality of a frightened Midwestern snake-oil salesman operating far from home. We demand that our leaders be genuine and authentic. We expect them to be human, humble, and of good humor—to be and to act *real*.

And then there is the difficult matter of resonating with people, of being real in a shared emotional experience. Without question, our crisis leader must have empathy for those experiencing hurt, loss, or shock. The word "empathy" derives from German, connoting "feeling into." Except for those suffering empathy-deficient conditions such as certain forms of autism, we all know what it means to "feel into" others and experience their pain. But more than empathy is required.

In the midst of facing a Rogue Wave, empathy can cause complications and, perhaps, distraction. There is the unequivocal and hard expectation of leaders to engage in a crisis by putting a priority on action and direction. Empathy cannot get in the way or override the critical leadership functions of sizing up the situation, preparing a response, and making tough decisions.

Paul Bloom, Professor of Cognitive Science at Yale, clarifies this by reminding us that although empathy is what makes us human, it's not what makes us moral—or tough-minded. We can mirror the experiences of others, but walking in another's shoes doesn't necessarily aim us in the right direction. Where empathy is instinctive, we need moral reasoning to help us make the best choices.[37] It's just not enough to feel others' pain. We need to have good judgment.

Sometimes we call this balance of firmness and feelings *tough love*. We mean that leaders are to be both softhearted and hardheaded. Whatever they do, leaders shouldn't look for a way to shift blame. If the leader tries to rationalize the event while emergency efforts are under way, it's precisely the wrong formula: soft *headed* and hard *hearted*. It's as if labeling the perpetuators or victims of a disaster should take precedence over stopping their bleeding. Facing a Rogue Wave squarely, a viable and true leader leaves out any ramping up of guilt, shame, or remorse.

When President George W. Bush ducked and dodged after Hurricane Katrina, not taking decisive responsibility for delayed responses, he made bad matters worse. He stayed away from the scene, blamed state and local officials—and even the levees themselves. He defended his appointees and stonewalled later investigations into the failures. His behavior during Katrina reflected a personal leadership style, "a pro forma acceptance of responsibility, strong loyalty to subordinates, and a post-event conviction that the way it was handled did not require second guessing."[38] In the end, the public was not satisfied. The blamer-in-chief was blamed for mismanagement and negligence.

Winston Churchill, in contrast, offered a different formula. When met with surprise, he asked four questions to get to the bottom of things—in the first and last instance holding himself as accountable as anyone else:

- Why didn't I know?
- Why didn't my staff know?

- Why didn't they tell me?
- Why didn't I ask?[39]

Facing a Rogue Wave requires embodied action. Take decisive action, have empathy without vacillation, and assume responsibility without blame.

Don Sands, once a company incident commander for oil and gas drilling in the Gulf of Mexico, has seen many close calls on his watch.[40] When dangerous storms unexpectedly deteriorate and "wobble," they can kick up 50-foot high rogue waves. Don's job in such events was to evacuate workers from drilling platforms as safely as possible, by helicopter if feasible, but by boat, if necessary. When a platform catches fire, the rule is, "Get off now and don't try and fight the fire—the platform will be there tomorrow."

How does he think about emergencies and leadership behavior? It starts with calling the shots. He reveals he grew up in the Texas oil patch and can speak fluent "lease-operator," the language of manual work. In addition to being able to rub shoulders with the men, he says he always knew when to go into command and control mode. You need to know what you are talking about and you must have access to good data, but "you can't sit around."

He witnessed a horrific helicopter crash on a platform back in 1978 when an entire crew of his friends died. He lives with the memory. His rules: Get out of harm's way early, observe safety first, and allow no second-guessing from higher-ups. In other words, face it! An After Action Review can be accomplished later.

Naming, facing, and embodying—these are leadership tasks and qualities that require a high quotient of emotional intelligence. We asked Jan Johnson, president of Learning in Action Technologies, a leading expert in the arena of emotional intelligence, for her advice about how leaders behave most effectively in a crisis. Are there any rules of thumb?

My initial thought on this topic is that having the capacity to notice and name feelings is foundational to emotional intelligence. The confusion is in whether you express them or not. We do not advocate expression because that is so context driven. Whether you express them or not, you gain the gift of each feeling, the balance, and the wisdom the feelings provide. Notice and name them is the key to access the wisdom and direction feelings provide.[41]

"Notice and name" on the individual level corresponds to "face it and name it" on the organizational stage. Johnson confirms that there is a leadership imperative here. Leaders would do well to delve into the skills and behaviors for facing and naming truth and reality, not as a formula but as a predisposition for effective crisis leadership.

Hell's bells! Our aim is to increase your odds, Captain. But it's really up to you.

3

The Dark Night of the Soul: When Leaders Help Themselves

In a real dark night of the soul, it is always three o'clock in the morning, day after day.

—F. Scott Fitzgerald, *The Crack-Up*

Janice Lachance, once President Clinton's director of the U.S. Office of Personnel Management (OPM), recalls an incident that caused both organizational turmoil and personal anguish.[1] An employee at OPM was shot and killed on her way home from work while holding her baby in her arms. The victim had worked in Janice's office.

"It was utterly horrific."

An early recruit for a progressive welfare-to-work program at the agency, the employee represented the program's highest intentions. She was a hard worker with a great reputation and future. Her death reminded people of the closeness of violence in their lives. As for the program, it had endured partisan fights when it was created and now it was visible and open to criticism again. Could "these people" succeed in the workplace?

It was a Rogue Wave. Janice, in the epicenter of the storm, had to lead while grieving.

Your adrenaline starts to flow. You can't come apart because everyone else is coming apart. You reach deep down inside. I went to the funeral, the wake. I cried in both those places. That was all I could do (personally). I also didn't want it to become about me . . . I didn't want that. It wasn't about losing my

assistant or my friend. It was about her. I wanted people to deal with their rela-
tionship with her and not her role at OPM. I wanted to find and give everyone
reason for this. You could not find a reason why she was shot. But hopefully her
coworkers could answer the question, why did she come into our life?

The missing chapter in most emergency handbooks is the one about the leader's personal concerns, confusions, crossroads, and cruxes. Generals, department heads, team leaders, and shift supervisors all, some-day, suffer through a *dark night of the soul.*[2] Leaders typically feel they must put their needs on hold in order to do the job. But leaders aren't exempt from darkness. There's no escape or hiding from existential angst in a Rogue Wave.

When Alison Whitacre and her business partner discovered an employee in their small construction business had embezzled a sizable chunk of money, she felt as if she had been assaulted.[3] "I couldn't believe it. She was such a thoughtful person, knew my kids and always had candy on her desk for them." Alison's personal code of trusting and investing in people had been invalidated; she questioned who she was.

A number of tough-minded, experienced, mature, successful leaders whom we interviewed—people who could stare down a bear—told us about breaking down and crying outside the glare of public scrutiny. Others told us they felt dazed, bewildered, saddened, angered, anxious, and more.

The most poignant moments in our research were when a leader would stop the story and say, "I don't want to go there—my feelings are just below the surface," or "I have never told anyone the full story." And the full story was often an event that occurred years ago. Leaders frequently referred to *compartmentalizing* their fright and fear, anguish and grief. They have hidden their hurt from everyone except their partners, from every venue but their pillows. When followers are looking for any sign of frustration or flinching, coping with catastrophe is a double duty: attending to others while stifling one's feelings. Doing today's job is tough enough, never mind putting energy into stalling personal needs for later.

On the face of it, a Rogue Wave is terrifying. Those it washes over are bat-tered, bashed, bruised, or worse. It's a time like no other. In the maw of the storm, questions are universal. "Will I live? How will this affect my family? What should I do? How will I get through this? Why did this happen?" Answers are no more forthcoming for a leader than for anyone else.

Meanwhile, everyone wants something from leadership: "Help!"

When external demands crowd out soulful truths, leaders need help, too. And while it's no small challenge for crisis leaders to be good stewards of themselves in a storm, avoiding such work has significant consequence. The risk in not facing the Rogue Wave—as a person—is in not being able to heal or to lead. Such internal barriers will ultimately impede self-knowledge and prevent wholeness of outlook and spirit.

Resilience

Writing during the worldwide financial meltdown of 2008, two McKinsey directors concluded: "The future will belong to companies whose senior executives remain calm, carefully assess their options, and nurture the flexibility, awareness, and resiliency needed to deal with whatever the world throws at them."[4] And, since 2008, the world has continued to throw commercial and economic crises at senior executives, and much more. The morning digest includes stories of terrorist acts, natural calamities, political failures, pandemic diseases, environmental threats, random violence, and unexpected negative events of all kinds.

While external crises compound, leaders are confounded, needing to help others while feeling ragged and raw. They are of no use to their organizations if they're incapacitated by stress. Organizational viability, jobs, careers, livelihoods, and lives are at stake. Their ability to understand and act—to name the wave and respond at the helm—depends on *resilience*.

But resilience isn't always manifest or forthcoming.

The risk analyst and philosopher Nassim Taleb categorizes many of these occurrences as "Black Swans"—rare events, extreme in their impact, and predictable only in retrospect. His thesis is that humans are blind to randomness. We're wired to find patterns that are not there and miss seeing those that are. We, and the systems we create, are therefore fragile.[5]

Then when we're caught up short, we're likely to dodge responsibility, digging us in deeper. "The mind yearns for consonance" according to the science writers Carol Tavris and Elliot Aronson. It rejects disconfirming evidence of our convictions. When mistakes were made, our attitude is that it is not about me! It couldn't have been me! We opt for arrogance, making more failure, more likely.[6]

If only we could do better when responding to unwelcome news, confess when we've blown it, and somehow immunize ourselves against tomorrow's headlines! We clearly have an inkling that we should. We note that Amazon features more than 5,000 books about resilience.

In common usage, resilience means two seemingly opposed things: flexibility and rigidity. We call it resilience when we spring back from hardship (we are elastic), and then get back in the saddle and get on with things (we are tough). The incongruity of the word's meaning (bending but unbendable) gives it depth and power. The American Psychological Association defines resilience this way:

> Resilience is the process of adapting well in the face of adversity, trauma, tragedy, threats, or even significant sources of stress—such as family and relationship problems, serious health problems, or workplace and financial stressors. It means "bouncing back" from difficult experiences.[7]

Although resilience is ordinary and prevalent according to the APA,[8] it is also complex and dynamic.[9] People respond to Rogue Waves in varied ways. Leaders can be more or less resilient at work than they are at home. And they may be more or less resilient depending on whether the crisis is an unbidden Rogue Wave or has their fingerprints on it, making them feel implicated. Resilience is hard to nail down and even harder to predict.

The good news is that resilience is not a *given* in our makeup. It's not a trait. Instead, resilience is something we can improve. The APA says, "It involves behaviors, thoughts, and actions that can be learned and developed in anyone."[10]

So, resilient leaders are made, not born, and they can always get better at playing a bad hand. Our response to what happens to us matters more in terms of resilience than what actually does happen. If we want to pick up the pieces and persevere after a setback, we can do that. It's up to us to reframe unwelcome events in a way that gives them meaning. We can give ourselves credit for toughness when there's scar tissue, compassion when we've been hurt, and wisdom from having been there and learned. Down but not yet out, we can choose to dust ourselves off and move on.

Karen Reivich and Andrew Shatté have written in *The Resilience Factor* that the chief obstacles to resilience are cognitive.[11] They describe useful skills, such as examining assumptions and "cognitive reframing," that really work.

Harry uses resilience methods when coaching executive clients. One leader, "Mary," felt her supervisor wasn't making enough effort to understand her difficult and complicated job. What she told Harry revealed cognitive errors. She had made an assumption that because her boss had powerful backing from above, she had nowhere else to turn when she was in difficulty. Feeling stuck, she foresaw catastrophe and was considering finding a new job.

Harry challenged Mary's untested assumption about having no recourse and offered a no-doom scenario. Mary accepted the idea of reframing the problem, went back to her boss, and found him to be reasonable and willing to learn.

Reivich and Shatté conclude: "All of our lives have twists and turns but with resilience you can thrive no matter what obstacles you face. By changing the way you think, you can change your life for good."[12]

Organizational Resilience

Given the unknowns and variables in upheaval, a leader can never be fully prepared, never completely ready, and never be assured of resilience. The APA explains:

> *Disasters such as hurricanes, earthquakes, transportation accidents or wildfires are typically unexpected, sudden and overwhelming. For many people, there are no outwardly visible signs of physical injury, but there can be nonetheless an emotional toll. It is common for people who have experienced disaster to have strong emotional reactions .... Following disaster, people frequently feel stunned, disoriented or unable to integrate distressing information. Once these initial reactions subside, people can experience a variety of thoughts and behaviors. Common responses can be: Intense or unpredictable feelings ... Changes to thoughts and behavior patterns ... Sensitivity to environmental factors ... Strained interpersonal relationships ... [and] Stress-related physical symptoms.*[13]

The buck must stop somewhere, and leaders' obligations *as leaders* place the physical and psychological welfare of others first, even at their personal risk. Norman Augustine doesn't let leaders off the hook. "The one aspect of business in which a chief executive's influence is measurable is crisis management. Indeed, the very future of an enterprise often depends on how expertly he or she handles the challenge."[14] Concerted action is required. Captain and crew are sailing the same ship, which raises a pertinent question: Can the organization be made more resilient?

Judith Rodin, president of the Rockefeller Foundation, has collected stories of how communities and entire countries have bounced back after disruptions and have thereby realized a "resilience dividend"—greater capacities to react, recover, and revitalize.[15] She puts her finger on the need for collective, even global, resilience.

The U.S. military sets a standard for organizational resilience. Its legendary keenness for training sets it apart in our society. Ingrained in military intelligence is to build strength by developing it first at the level of smaller units (fire teams/squads/platoons), so as to increase synergy and the probability of success. Muscle building—both physical and mental—quickens reflexes and helps fighters short-circuit laborious thought processes. Normal procedures are made rote. The strategy is to take as much distraction and fumbling off the table as possible so that intuition and improvisation are enhanced. Take the *knowns* out of the equation so the *unknowns* can be met with maximum creativity, thereby increasing the possibilities for resilience.

To boost our knowledge about institutional resilience, scholars and experts have identified organizations in high-risk industries where accident prevention is built into predictive systems, management routines, and work culture. Examples include aircraft carriers, nuclear plants, and drug factories. Yet even among the best-run organizations, "normal accidents"[16] as well as Rogue Waves occur.

For organizations to be more stable and predictable, they need to be "sensemaking" bodies, according to Karl Weick.[17] Organizational sensemaking is akin to mindfulness—continuous attention to experience in the present moment—one of the essential elements of high reliability organizations (HROs), where accidents are statistically rare.

If errors are inevitable even in HROs, being mindful about prior mishaps is shrewd. Correct them before they worsen. Resilience, after all, is cure not prevention. Managers in HROs "take pride in the fact that they spend their time putting out fires."[18] Christian Moore, a therapist, counsels: "I found it to be much more productive to focus on the action—the next successful one second, and then another second, and another—than sitting around talking, planning and thinking about it."[19] Resilient leaders in resilient organizations take earnest, immediate action and "question what is happening rather than feign understanding."[20]

Of course, action presumes an ability to act. The leader must survive.

The Oxygen Mask

When Martha was working in the Obama Administration leading the General Services Administration, she was given an elaborate HAZMAT head-and-shoulder cover for use in the event of disaster. It was stowed in a drawer close at hand. Few beyond the organization's senior executives were issued such equipment. It was an awkward arrangement. "If the chemicals don't kill me," one executive joked half-heartedly, "the organization certainly will when all the people claw the hood off." The equipment reeked of privilege for the powerful. Nevertheless, the policy is grounded in common sense.

Safety procedures on commercial flights instruct able-bodied passengers to secure their oxygen masks before helping others. For those in positions of collective responsibility, it's neither selfish nor self-indulgent to attend to personal safety. Frankly, it's a matter of organizational survival. Continuity of authority and clarity of responsibility are imperative, and no entity that respects and relies on its leaders wants them endangered. Leaders do little good for themselves or their organizations if their well-being is compromised.

Leadership stories that celebrate bravery, loyalty, or even honor are considered heroic. President Theodore Roosevelt is known to have delivered an hour-long, whistle-stop campaign speech after being shot in the chest. (He lost the election anyway). Today, our perspective is that leaders who endanger themselves heedlessly are considered hubristic. Furthermore, a Rogue Wave says *no* to management trends such as "invisible leadership" and "self-managing organizations." Leadership must be viable in an emergency, and preserving the leader's health and welfare is an informed strategic choice.

What does it mean for a leader to find help? How can such support be wrung out of a Rogue Wave?

When the organization is scrambling to survive, there's little interest in meeting a leader's personal needs. This means you have to lead yourself and care for yourself. You have to give yourself permission to seek help if you need it. You also have to access who you are and tap your inner resources. A Rogue Wave event is not a good time to assume that someone else will notice you, read your mind, feel what you feel, and step in to rescue you.

There's an ocean of self-help guidance available to leaders. Disaster response is a popular subject. Since the events of September 11, 2001, the world has accelerated the study of crisis management and pursued it on a broad scale. Leaders have ample access to this information.

Our goal is not to offer you a comprehensive inventory of activities to minimize your risk, protect yourself, or surface the support you will need. Instead, we advocate a thesis that can guide and shape whatever particular actions are appropriate for you when the lights go out and you find your soul in the dark. Simply put: *Strength lies within.*

We are intrigued by the approaches and attitudes of leaders who reach inside.

In our experience, research, and conversations with leaders, we've been struck with how well they do two things:

- They frame the challenge adaptively. They see themselves as agents not victims.
- They ask for help. They see themselves as learners not victors.

We make the positive assumption that leaders (like most of humanity) possess a well of emotional and spiritual resourcefulness that they never fully plumb. Effective self-help is self-discovery. Rather than look for answers outside, we urge a reverse course: Clear the channels and look inside.

What stuff are you made of? How did you get that way? What are your gifts? How have you handled sudden, spontaneous, and significant challenges in the past? How might you crack the code on your internal locks and reach inside for purpose and meaning?

Leaders don't need to be outwardly dependent. They needn't sit in the breakdown lane flagging passers-by when there's an electronic link in the dash, a mobile phone in the console, a tire and set of tools in the trunk, a first aid kit in the glove compartment, and other passengers! More is within grasp than we might assume. Leaders who turn to their best selves, who truly lead themselves, can go some considerable distance in addressing their own needs. Much help is on the way, if you pick up a mirror and look for it there.

Calm Yourself

In the crush of the crisis, there's little time and much consternation. Panic feeds on panic, pointing toward chaos. Refusing to join the stampede even in some small way is a startling gesture and a sign of personal leadership. It's a brave soul who insists on calm in the midst of calamity.

Dr. Bessel van der Kolk, professor of psychiatry at Boston University School of Medicine and medical director of the Trauma Center in Boston, explains that significant distress "robs you of the feeling that you are in charge of yourself."[21] A person can lose the confidence needed for "self-leadership," which can be deeply undermining and a double loss—you're less sure of your capability to make decisions in your job, or your life. Do you dare influence others if you can't manage yourself?

You need to begin by getting a grip and calming yourself.

We heard as many ways to quiet down as we had interviews: praying, meditating, and surrendering to faith; turning to loved ones, mentors, and trusted associates; redoubling physical exercise and getting in shape; examining diet and drugs; employing all manner of positive self-talk; and surprisingly, *increasing* activity.

Our bodies are in the crisis with us. We know how our hearts pound, our skin flushes, and our limbs tremble in the face of difficulties. When adrenaline compels us to action, and when leaders pour themselves into simply *doing something*, this instinctive, gut reaction can be adaptive. Activity both gets things done and releases pressure. Manic behavior in the first phase of a disaster is one way to manage anxiety. It can be self-soothing.

Steve Lynott was a co-owner of a Washington-based consulting firm in the 1990s when the order-board completely collapsed.[22] He spent the entire long Easter weekend "calming" himself by tearing through every single one of the firm's invoices and expenditures. It was productive activity. It created a view of the current state of the business, and it helped manage his anxiety. "I dug into the numbers; five years of invoices; 600 invoices; and I coded them for patterns and insights . . . When you are under tremendous pressure you hit some synapsis that otherwise you don't reach."

Ginger Lew was part of the leadership team at the General Counsel at the U.S. Department of Commerce when Secretary Ron Brown and 34 people were killed in a plane crash.[23] The tragedy was enormous, stunning the organization and the entire government.

Lew was out of Washington when it happened, and she flew back as quickly as possible.

She was in shock and grief, and yet she found that being in action was her best option. She jumped immediately into the unprecedented legal tangles and protocol issues that emerged as she struggled to find a way to work within the laws of the land and according to the laws of the heart.

"How are families being notified? How will the remains be transported back? Who will represent the Administration at the funerals? Who pays for that? What about insurance claims?" Finding the answers was important in steering the organization in the immediate aftermath of the crash. Lew also found great personal relief in simply distracting herself with the work.

Many professionals such as pilots, firefighters, and surgeons have routines and techniques to focus themselves and take care of basic procedures. The effect can be a boost of clarity, confidence, and calm.

Recall Captain Chesley "Sully" Sullenberger, who landed flight 1549 on the Hudson River on January 21, 2009, after three minutes and twenty-eight seconds of powerless flight. Once the plane had stopped, he matter-of-factly ensured that all passengers were safely out on the wings or loaded into boats. Only then did he leave the plane. He has since been lauded as both a hero and an astoundingly calm and unpretentious leader. One of the six officials who first heard the flight recording exclaimed, "That guy has been training for this his whole life."[24]

Shaking off the shock is mostly an icebreaker, a warm-up act. Good training is invaluable in the early rush of a crisis. But a leader must also find something beyond immediate busyness as self-care. A Rogue Wave can require concerted, prolonged recovery—the full extent of its bruising might not appear immediately. The imprint on body, mind, and soul can be indelible. Leaders need a sustaining way of keeping calm and collected.

Past is now ruptured from present. There was a person before the event and there is a person after the event. But they are not the same. You're no longer the person you once knew.

In the wake of her very public political crisis, Martha could barely open a newspaper. She was on edge about seeing another article swiping at her or the agency she had been leading. She knew she was not entirely herself, the person she was familiar with. Her rational and emotional brains were not in their former balance. The public scandal, job loss, and congressional hearings she had experienced had put her in a state of extreme anxiety. Seeing her name in print caused her stomach to tighten and competing dialogues to begin looping in her head.

Other people in similar circumstances might react the same way, or perhaps do the opposite and shut down, become sluggish, and feel numb. Martha knew what was happening because her rational brain could observe and understand, but it could not banish emotional responses. She was faced with the postcrisis tasks of rebalancing neural connections.

Clueless about the underlying biology or physiology, Martha recognized she was in unfamiliar and uncomfortable territory. Distractions like watching TV did not move things along. Crying or complaining only left her further depleted. Plenty of people had suggestions for her, some patronizing and self-administered but others quite creative. She took a number of them to heart and gave them a try. The experimental and innovative side of her was intrigued. "Heaven knows I had nothing more to lose."

- She began voice lessons and was coaxed forward by a generous teacher. Singing is hard work, requiring the counterintuitive discipline of breathing from a strong core while loosening and opening the throat. The physicality of vocalizing was deeply relaxing even as it was perplexing. The ultimate effect was that her voice grew stronger, more powerful, and importantly, confident.
- She returned to an old hobby of making quilts. Color and geometry distracted her looping thoughts and replaced them with musings about visual

puzzles and optical illusions. Instead of meditating when she is on edge, she can close her eyes, consider a swath of colors and shapes, and enter a different realm of concentration.

- A friend brought her a light blue polished stone to hold in her palm, and they stood together in the garden and spoke of the loss of her work and work friends. Over time, she learned more about how to acknowledge loss out loud to others, ultimately writing a book and speaking to students and others.

Bit by bit she reestablished internal connections and external contacts.

Each crisis leader has to find or build her unique repair kit. Leaders can take heart in their commitment to innovation, experimentation, and the search for an ever better way. These leadership traits and impulses are adaptive in a crisis and may be critical to recovery.

Leaders who found and created a personal, self-care response exhibited personal curiosity in exploring others' ideas and experiences, and they seemed to know what simple acts such as breathing, chanting, focusing, exercising, and being mindful could do for them in their suddenly chaotic lives.

Know Yourself

Reverberations from Rogue Waves ricochet, linger, and endure. Attending to physical health is foundational for moving forward. Without it, emotional and spiritual work is stunted and starved.

But what's the next circle of support to restore a leader's personal balance? Obviously there's no formulaic answer, but there *is* universal agreement. The leader needs *self-awareness*: the ability to go deeply within, the skill to observe your behavior, and the discernment to know what truly makes you tick. Only you know best—what's most troublesome, what's been lost or changed, and what's needed in terms of your well-being.

Navel-gazing is neither vain nor silly. Out-of-touch leaders present unknown risks to their organizations due to impaired judgment and crippled instincts. They may miss insidious problems hiding in plain view, focus on restoring what's irredeemable, or fail to realize their own injuries. Such distortions can yield wildly misguided reactions and presage subsequent trouble.

The task is to establish safety and create order, not open up new fronts that extend the chaos. Leaders unaware of the seductive power of their personal demons or the mortal danger in their personal blind spots can't be trusted. A Rogue Wave is not an invitation to fulfill delusions of grandeur.

Self-aware leaders trust their gut, register immediate impressions, and credit spontaneous reactions. They get to do what they do best—solve problems.

Furthermore, leaders are more likely to absorb the asymmetry of a Rogue Wave when they realize their personal limits. A sharper understanding of the off-kilter situation they face frees their predilections to form new partnerships and engage the community—to do whatever is needed to survive. Steve Denne left the American Red Cross to join Heifer International as the chief operating officer in 2007.[25] His timing was impeccably bad. He thought he was joining a thriving organization that would continue on the same slope: ten straight years of growth. Instead, within six weeks of his arrival the global financial crash ripped into the philanthropic world and caused the organization to lose eighty percent of its revenue. Luckily, Steve's decades with the American Red Cross gave him business skills for handling a Rogue Wave. And his self-awareness was steadying.

> *On a personal level it was about being really, really, really super clear about values and how they would be manifested—my values—and showing how that aligned with organizational values. I told my assistant, "We'll cling to the high road, even if holding on by our fingernails."*

Steve's clarity about how deeply he was aligned with Heifer's values helped him make choices that inspired others. Self-awareness is leadership's first line of defense. Having done a personal inventory is like knowing your source code—especially important when your job requires self-sufficiency and aplomb.

In yoga there's a line between pain and stretch. Experienced practitioners know when a position is too hot or when it's reached a point where it can damage the body. They monitor the lines between making healthy headway and suffering distress. Sometimes we need the help of a physical therapist or an executive coach, but we are always dependent on our senses to discern the difference between a flash of pain and a good stretch.

In times of crisis, leaders need acute self-awareness in order to calibrate how much they can take on and how to move forward. Naming and facing an external crisis is a preeminent and profound leadership task, and so it is with naming and facing the crisis within.

Reclaim You

Soon after resigning from the Obama Administration and suffering through two highly charged congressional hearings, Martha made a critical and self-sustaining decision. She pulled out the draft of a novel she had worked on in the past, finished it, polished it, and published it. Online reviews have been enthusiastic, but of more importance to Martha was the proclamation of self that had always been there and her new identity as a novelist.

> In Our Midst *is completely and totally mine. I wrote it, I own it, and I made it happen. It came from me. In many ways it was a way of saying back to the world that I was not smeared or diminished by the scandal. I have a voice, I have a story, and I can generate more. I exist in ways you did not imagine.*

We interviewed the police chief Russ Laine, who doubted his effectiveness as a leader after a terrible departmental crisis.[26] Chief Laine reclaimed his capabilities through conversations with others:

> *I'm not looking for an answer. My conversation allows connecting, allows me to hear the words, allows me to analyze what I'm talking about it. Once you share a burden with someone else you only have half the burden. I'm still responsible for the department or what happened but it's that sharing ability that allows me (not to) feel all by myself, not isolated . . . It's a significant difference . . . It's good for me to talk about these things. You get to cast yourself as a main character.*

Similarly, Renae Conley, a former executive at Entergy, told us about an early and formative organizational crisis in her professional life.[27] She was responsible for investor relationships when her firm faced a hostile takeover. The grueling work was compounded by a fierce public battle that played out in the press. In the ensuing, intense, hundred-hour-work weeks, she claimed her leadership. "I discovered something in myself to push through it and work through it and never give up. I made my bones through that process."

Reclaiming can mean revisiting your relationship with how you work. Greg Temple was an executive at Avery Dennison when the financial Rogue Wave of 2008 rolled across the world's economy.[28] Greg's organization viewed the world in a structured way, preparing for likely contingencies and building budgets to grow incremental revenue. "The game every year is feathering the edges with not too much risk—grow a little bit."

When the 2008 crash hit, the notion of growing in a steady way simply looked like the other side of Alice's looking glass. Their business, like so many others, entered a free fall. The firm and its leadership had to adjust drastically, and they had to upend their usual approach to making decisions:

What worked for the team and me was to say: "This crisis is unfolding in a non-linear way around the world; some places are locked up and some places are just grim. So the marching orders are that you should act as if you are running the family business in your country."

The usual process for orchestrating planning turned into decentralizing responsibility and requiring personal judgment. "For much of our corporate lives we try to compel people into breakthrough mode, to summon the courage to make change," Greg told us. "Now, we're running for our lives."

While running, Greg evolved into a different leader.

Previously I saw my role as pushing people forward. Then it became more of a supporting role. My role was to explain the new rules of order. I became a facilitator.

I can't say today I'm wiser. I still go into herding mode, trying to get people to an answer. But in this case I didn't know the answer, so I gave everyone the space to see it coalesce.

Greg admitted that his "discomfort was extraordinarily high." The new way of working required a particular frame of mind: listen, invite, take in, and look around. "Everyone is always looking up to find God, but you must look down," so sayeth a nun. "God is so humble, he is under your foot."[29]

Reassert Your Purpose

A rogue wave will peel a forecastle from a boat. A financial meltdown will peel the balance sheet from a company. A bomb at the end of a marathon will peel a sense of invulnerability from a nation. While much is lost in disaster, much is revealed: the strength of a hull, the intangible assets of a company, or the underlying values of a democracy. A crisis can expose what matters most in an organization and leader: core purpose and the answer to the seminal question, "Why do I/we exist?"

For some, purpose comes from a sense of perspective and a calling. Remembering his grandfather, who worked on the railroad for 90 hours per week, and his father, who fought on Iwo Jima, Dylan Taylor, CEO of Colliers International, views leadership as an honor.[30]

Patrice Nelson, executive director of Urban Ministries of Durham in North Carolina, a community shelter and food pantry, is expressly clear about her purpose.[31] An MIT graduate who is also African American and an ordained minister, Patrice moved to Durham from Philadelphia to start over after a recent divorce and a fire that had destroyed her home and possessions. Patrice was motivated by her belief that "All people were created to do great things," and she was searching to do something truly helpful. She headed into a Rogue Wave.

On her first day on the job, she learned that the organization was running a $267,000 deficit with a budget that would soon increase it to $500,000. She discovered unethical behaviors, unprofessional attitudes, unaligned policies, and instances of unfair treatment. Confronting these problems, she made herself a lightning rod for criticism and accusations, including charges of racism. Her board of directors gave her a performance review that was positive but contained adverse feedback from her staff. "I don't like it," she remembers thinking, "but it won't kill me."

Patrice held on and stepped up. She began to correct past practices that had sanctioned people living in a shelter for years and years. "They can do more," she believed. Patrice replaced the old story of her agency—"three hots and a cot," with a goal to end homelessness in Durham. Now with a new story, new staff, new rules, new programs, and increased private donations, urban Ministries of Durham is healthier than ever.

I really felt this was where I was supposed to be. That kept me going. I wanted a faith-based perspective but not a church. I wanted something that was working with people in transformation. It felt like a calling. There was this sense of purpose.

Knowing or returning to one's purpose in leadership or life is deeply effectual when there's no way home—or if your home had been in the path of a storm. Purpose is *you*—it's yours—and it's out of harm's way. Purpose answers *why?* Why me, Lord? Why am I being tested? Why was I chosen? Why do I matter? Why do I deserve to be loved/needed/respected?

Leadership purpose has become a subject taught in business schools and company-based education programs, thanks to the groundbreaking work of Bill George, former CEO at Medtronic and now Harvard Business School professor. For George, purpose is *True North*, the directional side of what it means to be an authentic leader. "Without a real sense of purpose, leaders are at the mercy of their egos and narcissistic vulnerabilities."[32]

Harry is a student of George's teachings. He's taken seriously the self-scrutiny required to identify his leadership purpose and distill it into as few words as possible. His chosen words summarize both *how* he works with others as a coach and consultant and *why* he loves his career: "My purpose is to help people get out of their own way."

Harry is delighted when people remove impediments in their thinking and move on with their lives. When they try a new, perhaps unexpected behavior—such as admitting a mistake or a change of mind in a staff meeting—and find that it wasn't so hard to acknowledge and actually worked to their benefit, Harry feels his purpose is being served. The reason it suits him is that he knows how it feels *to be in his own way.* He has plenty of stories to tell about mistaken perceptions, illogical pursuits, and wrong-headed assumptions of his that needed to be excised (or exorcised) before he could move to a deeper place or to higher ground.

Reassert your purpose in times of muddle or struggle. When the compass has gone overboard, you can still find your True North.

Encircle Yourself

No amount of penchant, panic, or pride can justify a leader going it alone. Isolation is bad strategy. A lone wolf is a wolf excluded from the pack, an animal whose life expectancy in the wild is short.

As family, neighbors, and colleagues, we share reciprocal covenants. We support each other when the chips are down because that's who we are and what we do. Help yourself; accept help; offer help. But don't take things for granted. Networks don't materialize out of the ether—they must be established and nurtured in advance. Elizabeth Dole, the former president of the American Red Cross, an organization devoted to managing crises, is quoted in Norman Augustine's "Managing the Crisis You Tried to Prevent":

> *The midst of a disaster is the poorest possible time to establish new relationships and to introduce ourselves to new organizations ... When you have taken the time to build rapport, then you can make a call at 2 a.m. when the river's rising and expect to launch a well-planned, smoothly conducted response.*[33]

Your network should include people on whom you can impose. And they should welcome your imposition. According to management scholars Heifetz, Grashow, and Linsky, leaders are best served by confidants who "care more about you than about the issues at stake."[34] Repeatedly, leaders talked to us about their circle support. Spouses and families often played primary roles.

Linda Rabbitt, founder and CEO of a construction firm in Washington, D.C., told us that when her partner who was a technical expert left the company she found herself feeling insufficiently skilled to handle the business. It was her husband who set her right.[35]

> *He could have said, "You are right and you are not cut out for this." Instead, he said, "Look at it this way, you are perfect for this service business ... You're Lee Iacocca. You don't know how to build the car, but you know how to sell it."*

She was so startled by what he had said, she still remembers the room she was in and where she was sitting. And the advice worked. Just like that Linda was ready to rejoin the fray. "My father was an automotive engineer with 19 patents—an engineer and a genius—but he only knew how to create, not how to sell. I can sell."

Michael Dukakis talked with us about tough times in his long life of public service.[36] As governor of Massachusetts, he recalled the Blizzard of 1978 when record snowfall in the Northeast killed a hundred people and caused billions of dollars in damage. Then there was the 1980s Massachusetts Miracle that faded, leaving everyone in the region "mad as hell." It wasn't the first time that, in the governor's wry words, he "took a pounding."

We asked how he was able to perform, to function, to continue on, year after year. The governor's answer came without hesitation. "I'm a steady guy," he said, who relied on his family for support. He abided by simple rules, such as "no politics on Sunday" and "be home for dinner at 6:00 pm." "I was fanatic about it. And I can't tell you just how important those two rules were and not just as a good father and husband, I mean they were important for *me*."

Beyond the family circle, networks can be especially supportive. When they're not just contacts for transactions, they can provide timely and relevant guidance. Sometimes the most significant help isn't expert support or problem solving—it's companionship.

Steve Piano, a human resources executive, was called in the middle of the night about a nightmarish event.[37] An employee had been killed in the company's parking lot. He drove immediately to the office to meet with law enforcement and begin communicating with employees. After twenty hours of nonstop work, Steve needed respite more than rest. He needed to talk to someone trusted who would understand the situation and simply listen. He found that listener in an HR colleague.

Family, friends and close colleagues are easily accessible, often nearby, and well acquainted with a person's moods and needs. They're also valuable in offering privacy. Leading a team during a crisis is highly visible. It's critical to be available and be seen. But leaders also need a circle of support that's neither in the circle of need nor in the circle of public view.

As leaders step into operational command centers and speak with the voice of confidence and authority to their people, paradoxically they become more vulnerable—now they have nowhere to run, nowhere to hide. And thus a new opportunity arises. Unrequested help often arrives. Openness to new ideas and an uncritical willingness to receive support are magnetic. When the leader is available and ready to listen, constructive messages or helping hands appear. And they can come from strangers.

During the Chilean mine disaster of 2010, André Sougarret intentionally invited ideas from all corners in order to rescue the men trapped deep underground. He knew the situation was unprecedented, and he was willing to have it revealed that his networks were slim.[38] An entourage of drilling experts arrived from around the world, and rescue was accomplished. Leaders can't rely only on those they already know, even on a good day. They benefit most from keeping their eyes on the prize, being agnostic about ideas and their origins, and giving credit where due.

An archetype for this unexpected support is the *angel,* a being who brings helpful messages from a (presumably) holy place, and like an angel investor, has only an advisory, noncontrolling stake in the outcome. Among other things, an angel figure is a reminder that there may be additional help and hope offered by people we do not know or know well.

We're reminded of travel, odyssey, and quest stories in which unexpected helpers appear along the way, often as unusual as they are wise, to play crucial roles. These helpers are ubiquitous in animal form in the stories of our childhoods, from Cinderella's helpful mice to Lassie, the dog that saves his owner from missteps. As we mature in our literary tastes, the helpers assume realistic human forms. Sherlock Holmes finds his Watson, Don Quixote his Sancho Panza, and Huckleberry Finn, the motherless son of a ne'er-do-well, is cared for and guided by the escaped slave, Jim. In a more recent text, the hero of Charles Frazier's novel, *Cold Mountain,* returning home from the Civil War, stumbles upon an old woman in the woods who offers him shelter so he can rest, recover from his wounds, and regain his strength.

Because these surprising helpers can be enigmatic, their messages might not register in more normal circumstances and their help might be rejected. When needs are great and the leader's ego is in suspension, a simple touch, a word, a token, a meal, or a sympathetic ear is freely proffered.

Harry has a story of such a moment. He had earned his doctorate and had a family to support. The only job he could find was as a bartender, a job he wasn't very good at. Panicking, he saw a job placement service listed in the *New York Times,* called the number, and surprised himself with what came out of his mouth.

"I'm worried I may not find a job," he said. It was a deeper truth.

The wise stranger at the other end of the line said: "What, you mean you aren't going to work ever again, for the rest of your life?" It hit a chord.

Harry's world was reapportioned immediately. His panic subsided; he soon found a job and began a career.

Another story about a deft touch is a moment he has never forgotten. During the war in Vietnam, Harry was attending divinity school and was deeply troubled by world events. At an informal gathering, he said to his dean, Krister Stendahl, a New Testament scholar, "If it could be that the world might come to an end—tomorrow—what difference does it make what we do today?"

Dean Stendahl's response: "And what if the world does *not* end tomorrow?" A single comment rearranged Harry's world.

Pre-Resilience

There may be one headed right your way right now—a Rogue Wave, that is. If your boat is small and your crew untested, how will you survive?

Your first job is to thrive as the person you *already are*.

A reservoir of accumulated clues and memories lies within. These sources of strength are unknown or unavailable to us unless and until we drill down and frack them, the bedrock that supports our identity. What got us here—our pat answers and unexamined assumptions about how the world works and our place in it—can't take us all the way to where we want to go.

The upside of upheaval is that we have to search for new answers. When Rogue Waves atomize internal resistance to growth and change, they're salutary. They illuminate your predicament. There is an inner glow of *pre-resilience*.

At such a time, messages we heard as youngsters or bits of insight from people we respect may float to the surface of our consciousness—often in a good way. We have ideas tucked away from previous experiences that are a treasure trove when we are under stress. Childhood lessons can suddenly emerge years later when we're in a tough spot. A simple line of a song, a word from a teacher, or a conversation at the water cooler can stick and pay off later.

Harry values a crystalline question asked him long ago. He told his supervisor he wanted to resign and take a job in another company. His boss asked, "Are you running toward or running away?" Ouch.

Although Harry was looking for an escape from what he judged were petty organizational politics, he confessed that his frustrations could be surmounted. Maybe what he needed most in that moment was just to complain and to *be heard*. Suddenly it wasn't at all clear what he was "running toward." Grateful for the speed bump that slowed a headlong rush for the exit, Harry stayed where he was for several more years and benefited in many ways.

Over the years, Harry has become used to asking himself big questions when it matters most. Are you being purposeful? Are you being courageous?

Are you being responsible? Self-scrutiny is now embedded in his nature when pushing through imponderables in the darkest hours of sleepless nights. And what he finds most interesting is that he finds it grounding—and even comforting—to go "to his core."

It's worth reflecting on how we react when we have been shocked. Where were you, on September 11, 2001? What did you do when the MRI showed a shadow? How did you react to the phone call about the car accident? Remember your response in that unforgettable moment in the boardroom, the convention center, or your office? You already know a lot about how you will face a Rogue Wave. Fate's fickleness needn't fool you every time, and you don't need a training session on resilience. Your *pre-resilience* is already part of you.

When Stephanie Streeter, former CEO of Banta, was challenged to defend her company from a hostile takeover attempt, she knew the deal would make money for the acquirer but be bad for her company.[39] She reverted to a personal pattern of problem solving she learned as a child when she would drive everyone in her family crazy with her steady stream of whys, wherefores, what-ifs, and how-abouts. "I was the question machine."

That curiosity—sometimes courageous—and her basic distrust of surface appearances served her well all through school, at Stanford, and then as a professional. It is no surprise that Stephanie's relentless investigation into the ins and outs of foiling unfriendly takeovers felt natural. She stayed focused on preserving shareholder value and chose a "white knight" solution in new ownership by R. R. Donnelly. In the three months in which these events unfolded there was no moment to spare, and Stephanie's pre-resilience was her go-to strength.

Rogue Waves require top-shelf responses such as courage and integrity. And they invite more modest but no less valuable moves such as being in tune with your motivations, being comfortable in your skin, and being aware of your impact on others.

Anne Kemp, a human resources director, returned to her office after lunch one day and found her boss waiting for her—with a cop.[40] Two detectives were there to inform her that her training manager was being charged with fraud in a sophisticated embezzlement operation in which Anne's name had been forged. They wanted to begin the execution of their responsibilities by having Anne take a lie-detector test. The afternoon promised to be awkward for everyone.

Anne remembers the story her mother used to tell her. "As an infant in the crib, I respected you as 'the competent one in the family.' " Both of Anne's parents had unflagging confidence in her. In school, as she earned straight A's; her dad often told her, "Keep up the good work." This stream of positive encouragement became elemental to her self-knowledge. "Everything got pushed through this frame [of self-confident achievement]."

Anne immediately agreed to take the lie-detector test. But then she went one better by asking for an additional exculpatory test, a handwriting analysis. In the company's engineering culture this was a strong move, indicating her faith in data and evidence, and putting to rest any possible doubts about her honesty or capability. Anne was completely exonerated. The culprit was dealt with, and her department got back to work.

In reflecting on this story, Anne shared one of her favorite quotations: "Good judgment comes from experience; experience comes from bad judgment." Be prepared for a Rogue Wave by knowing who you really are, and then be that person.

Everyone has self-edifying anecdotes. Some are like kōans—they teach volumes in just a few words. In a micro-story that has yielded lasting insight, Martha remembers a time when her husband caught his hand in the mixer. Although she did not see it, she heard it, whirled around and pulled out the plug. Martha learned in this quick moment about her ability to *hear* information, respond rapidly, and also make a decision about mechanics, even in a storm of surprise and fear. Simple stories yield such self-knowledge. Sometimes they're so elementary we don't realize their impact on our thinking.

Leaders have special responsibilities but no special magic or mojo in a Rogue Wave. Formally learned behaviors and absorbed observations of others can improve our odds. But success germinates from within.

The late James Hillman, a therapist and writer, quoted a line from the poet W. H. Auden, "We are lived by powers we pretend to understand." On some deep level, he explained, we have a sense, "almost primitive and naïve, that though the will be bankrupt and the heart in despair, you can never be all alone, never be powerless. Something has you always in mind."[41]

That *something* needs to be *you*.

4

Don't Just *Do* Something.
Be There! (For the Organization)

All we have to do is ask "How can I help?" with an open heart, and then really listen.

—Ram Dass and Paul Gorman[1]

On August 29, 2005, Hurricane Katrina delivered death, destruction, and dark nights to 37,000 square miles of southern Mississippi, Alabama, and Louisiana. Renae Conley was one among many thousands for whom the event was "life-changing."[2] As president and CEO of Entergy Louisiana and Energy Gulf States Louisiana, she was charged with restoring power for more than a million customers.

Entergy's transmission networks had been hit hard. "Everything was on the ground," said a lineman.[3] Entergy's workers and their families had been hit too, but they had to go to work for the good of all. Renae was accountable for the welfare of her recovery teams.

And she was also responsible for her family.

I'm still very emotional when I talk about it because of what you saw people go through on so many levels. The father of my son-in-law drowned, and my daughter had to live with us, so her kids had to transfer schools. I had people with so much emotional pain. My assistant lost everything: twelve feet of water in her house. She could never go back. I'm trying to advise her and she just can't make decisions. You're making a lot of personal decisions as well as business decisions.

The Cycle of Helpful Help

Figure 4.1

Renae's story exhibits a pattern we discovered in listening to leaders: Aiding people helped them endure. It's the golden rule in a continuous cycle of helping, receiving help, and growing as a helper. The cycle is depicted in Figure 4.1. Walking a mile in another's shoes resouls yours.

Ram Dass and Gorman write, "We work on ourselves . . . in order to help others. And we help others as a vehicle for working on ourselves."[4] Renae suffered. She gave—and she gained though giving.

You're processing a lot of things. You have to be in control emotionally because people are struggling with their own losses and how to put things back together. You're trying to help everyone else put one foot in front of the other. "Here's what we have to do today." You're the front line. Nothing really happens until the light gets back on. You're the utility. On the other side of it . . . people have to be relocated, (you) have to bring them back. They're lots of different dimensions of what you're trying to put together to keep moving forward.

So I think that for me it was a lot of reflection on what you really value. I came out the other side of it really understanding myself and what was important in life. When you go through something like that and see so many losses, (you see life as) really pretty transient.

So, I was married, and coming out of it I ended up getting divorced, after 30 years of marriage. For both my husband and me it was a "what are you doing with your life?" moment. "Stuff" doesn't really matter. That's not what life's about. Are you happy? How do you want your life to go?

Renae helped others and was helped by others. The recursive cycle of giving and receiving help was her route to recovery.

So much for me was "how do I help them?" We had people in headquarters in Baton Rogue. They were working twenty-four-hour days, almost. We got massages for people. We got people to cut hair. It sounds silly but it was just "how do we help your life be a little more normal in the middle of the chaos?" A lot of times, it was "how did I help others just to maintain some level of normalcy among the chaos?" That's very healing.

It still chokes me up. There was a woman who worked for the company who didn't have a coat, so I gave her my coat. I saw her a few years later, and she said, "Do you remember giving me your coat?"

It's the little things that help you process and feel that you are making a difference. I'm a very spiritual person and I do believe that it wasn't like (we're) victims—we're going to work through this. You come out the other side of it.

Renae, and Entergy, and Louisiana moved through the Rogue Wave to higher ground. She emerged stronger and wiser. Work eventually became "more fun and rewarding."

My husband was black, so I had a very strong sense of fairness and treating people with respect, being interracially married. My life experience was that I was viewed as a minority, and so I had insight into different people and cultures. I always worked to realize that I happened to have a position and I wasn't a better person. That helped me be a better leader, really trying to trust people that they were doing the right thing . . . .

The CEO role was very political, and it was a regulated utility. I didn't agree with some people, but they became friends of mine. When you break it all down, you all want the same thing—it doesn't make them better or worse . . . .

I always look for what I like in people. I do have a really positive attitude towards life, and that when I worked to make sure that I'm connecting with this person, I'm finding what I like about them and we have to figure it out together to get something done. It was a much more powerful way to get things accomplished.

After Katrina, Renae was promoted to the corporate office of the chief executive to focus on the development of Entergy's people. Even today her words reflect her Katrina experience:

How do you still make a difference? You have some level of obligation when you have experiences and opportunities that have been given to you. How do you help other people?

The dark night of the soul is not just an individual condition. It's a condition *shared*. It is sad for everyone when neighbors' belongings are destroyed. It is grievous to all when lives are lost. The concept of community is now more than a sense of belonging to a neighborhood or organization—it has the added dimension of the awareness of mortality.

Leaders know that the physical safety of human beings requires their immediate attention. What follows next is focus on the spiritual, emotional, and psychological care of these same human beings. We call these combined responsibilities Helpful Help.

Helpful Help

James March, the organizational theorist (and published poet), wrote and taught for five decades about the quixotic dilemmas of making leadership decisions in a world full of ambiguity. The "practical problems of organizing meetings, giving orders, or whatever, are important," yet of an entirely different order than "fairly deep questions about 'the nature of trust' and 'the nature of love' " . . . that are "fundamental to being a leader or understanding leadership." For March, leadership is *both plumbing and poetry.*[5]

Helpful Help after a Rogue Wave resides in "fixing the plumbing" with a poet's sensibility. Helpful Help begins with the tasks of securing safety, providing aid, and making repairs, and proceeds from there. More than a set of answers, a list of activities, or a checklist of duties, it *goes beyond* just doing things. Helpful Help is never cast in the heroic mold in the sense of calling attention to itself, and it doesn't make the leader feel smarter, better, or more in control. Helpful Help is leadership that offers and receives humanity.

Michael Conforti's approach as a practicing therapist involves adopting a posture of *compassion* ("I see your suffering"), *empathy* ("I am affected by your pain"), and *humility* ("I can do little to combat the pain, but I can be with you").[6] His goal is to help a person reclaim membership in the human community, as a full person, not as a victim to be pitied or cast aside, but never to diminish his experience of pain. Leaders can emulate these behaviors.

Some leaders in our interviews and workshops would confess discomfort with Helpful Help. "It's too vague" or "It's too anxiety-producing." Or they might be thinking, "It isn't in the default setting of project management software," and anyway, "It's someone else's job." Leaders are rarely trained therapists, and they understandably fear making things worse. Their job is preparedness and response, not healing.

Without question, Helpful Help isn't straightforward. Offering Helpful Help challenges a traditional notion of leaders, which is to be in charge. Helpful Help confronts self-control as it is commonly understood and valued: coolness, reserve, and emotional steadiness.

The work of healing exists in a different framework than the exercise of authority and decision rights based on an organizational chart. The healing leader works *alongside* others in the organization, not solely from a position of power or authority. Recovery can't be commanded, but it can be supported.

Leaders also suffer during crises. They may be consumed with dismay, loss, and regret. Disasters can feel like accusations of failure. Importantly, under Rogue Wave conditions, the playing field for suffering is leveled. Human struggles are co-mingled, and nurture that is expressed for others via small gestures and acts of compassion becomes self-nurture.

Helpful Help is both mutual and reciprocal support. We are not lost. We are not alone. We are not devastated. I am here with you. You are here with me. What we share—our purpose, our care for one another—will carry us forward.

The meta-message of being there when it counts most is the promise of a better day in the future.

Be There

In an interview with Ben Cohen and Jerry Greenfield, the famous Vermont ice cream makers, Jerry was asked his definition of the word "friend." Jerry said,

> *That's easy: Ben. About a week ago, I fell down, hit my head, and gashed myself before a concert. I was on the floor, and Ben, being the good friend that he is, came and lay down on the floor next to me while I was recouping. It wasn't like "Are you okay? Can I help you?" It was like, "I'm going to lie down right with you."* [7]

Ben's demonstration of friendship is the posture of a leader bringing Helpful Help. It's rooted in the idea that a leader's value is first and foremost to *be there*! This implies being alongside people as a fellow human being, and communicating that you are impatient with ready answers and facile solutions. Be eager to be deeply involved in the organization *as a community.*

A leader can, at times like these, choose to ignore hierarchy and protocol. A gesture of affiliation may be as simple as going out for beer with the team or as significant as showing up in an emergency room or visiting victims' families. How it is done doesn't matter as long as the leader demonstrates caring and shows that the organization is not a house divided by pain, but a community brought together through misfortune. There is safety and reassurance in being together.

John Kim, a New York Life executive, insisted on team togetherness during the 2008 financial crisis and arranged for his group to work together out of a conference room. His father had been a pastor, and he had observed that in times of difficulties, parishioners would solve things together. In the financial crisis, his team members needed one another, and John needed them, too.

In the wake of September 11, 2001, a group of researchers published a report in the *Harvard Business Review* based on findings from a project known as CompassionLab. The research was sparked by interest in how acts of compassion can spread and compound, inspiring more acts of compassion. They studied organizational compassion and how it enables healing after crises.

> *A seemingly simple but important aspect of demonstrating your humanity is just being present, physically and emotionally. It shows employees that the organization cares about what will happen to them and will do whatever it can to help them in a time of need.*[8]

They add, "There is tremendous power in just sitting with people as they process terrible events."[9]

We can go even further. Be there and *listen*.

Early in Harry's graduate training he took a course in pastoral counseling where he learned just how hard it could be to listen. One of the assignments was to record a counseling session with a classmate. When it was his turn to be counselor, Harry's partner said only this: "I'm scared."

"About what?" Harry asked.

"I'm scared," came the reply.

"Can you say more?"

Same reply: "I'm scared."

Harry was flummoxed. To this day, he remembers the fright he experienced as he listened to this fear—whether or not it was fictitious or role-played.

When doctors listen, patients receive better care. Nirmal Joshi, chief medical officer for Pinnacle Health System, writes that over 70 percent of adverse health outcomes in hospitals are due to miscommunication and miscues, not technical mistakes. Nevertheless, doctors wait, on average, just 18 seconds before they interrupt patients who are narrating their concerns. As Dan Blazer, a professor of psychiatry at Duke University, observes: "Psychiatrists count symptoms, but patients tell stories."[10]

Listening requires time, a limited resource, but patients deserve patience! Joshi says, "A good bedside manner is good medicine."[11] And a good work-site manner is good leadership.

Peter Kramer, a professor of psychiatry at Brown University and the author of *Listening to Prozac*, describes his approach as "sitting beside the patient metaphorically and looking outward, handcrafting interventions on the spot." Extrapolating to times of collective hurt when a leader must lead, the prescription is to stand beside the organization, look beyond the present circumstance, and deal in real time with what people need.[12]

Sometimes the best medicine, the best advice, is none at all. William Doherty, a family therapist who teaches workshops for "marital first responders," writes about this finding in his research: "People who confide in a friend say it is most helpful if the friend simply listens."[13] Doherty explains that listeners can help by giving emotional support or providing a larger perspective, but offering more than that may make a listener seem judgmental or self-centered.

It is acceptable, Doherty advises, to reflect a person's feelings back to them, to make nonverbal contact that communicates caring attention, and to affirm a person's strengths. It is not useful to exude enthusiasm and encouragement if it results in a person feeling that they have not been heard.

Barry Dym, once a family therapist and now founder and executive director of the Institute for Non-Profit Management & Leadership Organizational Behavior, has counseled people in crisis over the years following this approach:

> First I make sure I don't have a plan right away. I listen, and then I find a way to continue two conversations. Practical: "What are you going to do?" And emotional: "How will you deal with this on an emotional level?"[14]

Leaders need not be therapists to appreciate how Barry would counsel them. Don't solve things for people. Listen to them. Really listen. And when you inquire, refrain from offering advice. You can't remove pain and suffering. You *can* be there by the side of the one suffering, You *can* hear them, and you *can* acknowledge what they say.

Denise Hudson was in charge of supply chain and quality functions of a pharmaceutical company in 2011. Just before Christmas, a Rogue Wave appeared.[15] Suddenly their main supplier of a critical drug was shutting down for quality reasons. This was a $650 million crisis for her company, and it presented a huge danger for customers who depended on the medicine. She and her team spent the holidays attacking the problem.

> *So we sped up validation, worked with people overseas, worked with the FDA for exceptions, and found other sources. We had some drugs people couldn't do without and needed special waivers. We had to work multiple and parallel paths at the same time. We talked daily, tracked every little detail. By March, all of our products were back in supply with about two-to-three weeks of stock on big ones.*

Denise included "a lot of people in thinking and processing things," listening to them carefully and deeply, while quieting self-blame and doubt.

She had learned to do this in a previous experience as a plant manager in the 1990s, where problems were piling up. Denise began receiving help from all sides and from some who accused her of ruining the plant. Her staff invited her to a meeting that became confrontational. They told her how awful everything was, and she listened—for five long hours. And, somehow, in the midst of all of this confrontation and negative messaging, a corner was turned. Her attitude was "you can't be in the middle of the ocean and decide you don't want to swim"—so they swam. Fifteen years later the plant is still alive and is a much better place to work than it was before her marathon listening meeting.

Denise has a deep belief that in a leadership role "you've got to involve the people . . . and they've got to feel they can tell you they think you're stupid." She benefited from "that pressure (of) being able to stand there and appear confident when sometimes inside you feel like, Oh brother! They needed to feel that I wasn't shaken." She couldn't fix the source of their frustration, but she could listen. And then, working together, everyone could fix the problems.

This is not a simple task, especially for leaders, eager to move quickly toward achieving results. Listening creates an open space in time. Although it seems counter-intuitive within the urgency and drama of a Rogue Wave situation, you should slow down now, in order to go faster later.

Greg Temple felt that pull and tug that comes from opening up to real listening when he was supply chain leader during the global financial crisis:

> *I found myself really struggling. We were setting up conference calls and video-conferences that were really well attended. During those times you would schedule a videoconference and ninety-eight percent of the people are there early because they want to know what the hell is going on.*
>
> *Minutes before you aren't sure, what am I going to say?*
>
> *I learned to listen more and make it more of a conversation: What's going on in this country or that country? It takes it immediately from a one-way to more of a community that is going through the storm together. It levels the playing field. If I learned anything, it was recognizing that filters don't help. Let's grapple more noisily together and we'll have a better answer, more agility.*[16]

When a leader listens, it opens doors for team members to engage, to feel less isolated, and to grapple noisily with the situation at hand. When despair is also in the room, the necessary listening may take the form of a handshake and a hug.

Be Smart—About Feelings

Helpful Help can be confusing. Isn't a leader supposed to appear strong and confident? And at the same time appear empathetic and genuine? How is a leader *supposed to feel*, and how much personal emotional truth can be revealed?

When Martha resigned from the Obama Administration, it was head-line news. While she tried to appear composed, she felt that anger "leaked out of me." She crafted her remarks to Congress carefully, aware that it was her last opportunity to say good-bye to her agency as they watched the hearings online. She wanted to be calm and positive, telling them once more how proud she was of their important work and innovations. Nevertheless, she could imagine a different speech, one she would have liked to give to Congress, one with the gloves off.

Two years later, when the *Washington Post* featured her in an article, she was more frank. The reporter who wrote the story had sought her out because of the openness Martha had displayed in writing about her experience, and she found that candor unusual for Washington. The title of the article was "Resigned." Some friends loved the directness. Others thought she was portrayed as falsely blue, while one wrote to tell her to quit wallowing in her sorrow. Martha still thinks about the entire series of events and the coming together and crosshatching of dignity, honesty, and (perhaps even) whining. She wonders what it looked like to others.

The recommended rule for communication during untoward events is transparency. Received wisdom is that "no bad news improves over time." Automatically, we say that the same must apply to emotions. Communication experts advise us that honesty is the best policy. But Helpful Help is not a concern about managing either a public image or a commercial brand. The aim and intent of Helpful Help is to develop and maintain genuine and restorative relationships both within an organization and with its stakeholders—relationships that affirm vulnerability and acknowledge the need to heal.

Importantly, people will talk openly about their feelings and reactions after a Rogue Wave has swept over them. Across studies of 1,384 emotionally significant episodes in organizations, more than 90 percent of those affected talked about it.[17] There is a secondary wave of street talk and hallway buzz. When people are disturbed, they will act upon the urge to tell others. They want meaning, they want the news, and their emotions become their personal or communal media.

In groups, whether news is positive or negative, if it is important to someone, it gets shared. So the next question for a leader is stark. Do you want to be a part of the conversation, or not? This is a time to help shape perceptions, direct the dialogue, and offer perspective. To back out of the chatter means to allow break-room and water-cooler conversations to proceed unedited, to take their own courses, and to create divergent narratives.

We presume you want to participate. If so, how much can you share about how you really feel? Is it safe to display your emotions?

Addressing the country about the Sandy Hook Elementary School killings, President Obama wept. He explained that he was moved, in great part, because of his feelings as a parent. "You're not alone in your grief," he said.[18]

During the Chilean mine disaster, there was crying among leaders, above and below ground. André Sougarret engineered the rescue of the thirty-three miners and eventually broke down and wept while on camera. "My objective has always been to unite the families with the miners and every time that it happened, it touched me," he said the next day. "I am a person, I believe in the family, I think it is necessary for them to be together, and every time that was fulfilled, it was a great feeling for me, hugely emotional."[19]

At the same time, leaders don't want to rattle a fragile situation in which people are desperate for calm. As Southern Methodist University's Frank Lloyd says, "You don't want to panic, yourself. You want people to think: That person knows what to do."[20] Leaders can't afford to fall apart. Emotional discipline is essential. Leaders have to exercise command over themselves in order to command others.

Nevertheless, especially in times of disaster, emotional management is tricky.

We present the case of Teresa Sullivan, the first woman president of the University of Virginia, who may be the "unluckiest president in America," according to *Fortune*. In a recent survey of the world's "50 greatest leaders" according to the magazine, Sullivan deserved an "A" in "rebounding from disaster." She's survived as president when there were undergraduate murders and student sexual assaults, a request from her board to resign, an explosive *Rolling Stone* article about a rape in a fraternity that has since been retracted, and a recent arrest that resulted in both the injury of a black student and the uproar of a campus in protest against it. Throughout, according to Sullivan, "The most important thing was how I behaved, not how I felt."[21] As an introspective person, she does not choose to show her emotional cards.

"There's a negative stereotype of women being overemotional and thus not able to lead," Sullivan told *Fortune*. Steadfast, rational, dispassionate, she is caught in a paradox—to appear to be the type of woman leader she hasn't chosen to be and display her feelings, or to stay as stoic as she has chosen to appear and suffer the consequences. UVA's student council president recognizes her qualities as an accessible leader, yet he says, she has "struggled to provide the emotional leadership that the community needs."[22]

Kristi Lewis (Tyran), a professor at Western Washington University, researched how followers respond when leaders display emotions.[23] She focused on the negative emotions of sadness and anger. Participants in an experiment viewed videos of male and female actors portraying a CEO delivering bad financial news and urging better performance to determine how viewers felt both about the situation and the effectiveness of the leader. What were the findings?

Emotional tone matters. In general, sadness depresses viewers and yields passivity, while anger excites others and stimulates action.

When the CEO actors showed sadness, they were downgraded in perceived effectiveness. Notably, there's another dynamic. When female actors showed anger, their ratings sunk. When males showed anger, their ratings remained the same. So, for women, showing negative emotions seems to be a lose–lose. Both sadness and anger may adversely impact perceptions of their leadership. For men, it's lose–stay even. Sadness works against them, but anger yields a neutral result. In neither case (it would seem) does it advantage a leader to cry or to yell.

What is the standard? On one hand, the leader is held to a different expectation than everyone else. If the organization's perception is that the leader is losing it, sobbing, or raging, the leader's competence will be questioned. And yet, negative emotions sometimes help organizations adapt, and help a leader lead—*if* the leader is trusted and *if* the story is plausible.

As Lewis writes, "Observing an emotion in a leader may help followers interpret ambiguous situations, such as a company experiencing problems."[24] More cues than words and numbers are needed to help us navigate meaning when we are confused. Unlike in experiments where respondents don't know the actors or care personally about the case, in actual situations with tangible consequences, where there is complexity and there are unknown or disputed facts, a leader's emotional state offers us inklings about how we should think and feel. This is no small matter. Our emotional brains are smarter and more capacious, by far, than our short-term memory banks with their conscious processes.

We conclude that the root issue concerning emotional display is not whether showing feelings is positive or negative, active or passive, but *whether the feelings are authentic and fit within a coherent narrative.*

Even though leaders may assume that their emotions are a part of what they bring to their leadership roles, it's common for them to be wary about showing feelings of any kind, and to be regretful when emotions burst forth—even love and joy!

Laboratory experiments conducted at Erasmus University in the Netherlands shed light on why leaders default to emotional opacity in moments of passion or pathos. When leaders aren't clear about the difference between *regulating* their emotions and *expressing* them, they often shut down completely. When they can't compute the interactions of their emotional state and the possible effectiveness of their message, they play it safe. The trouble is, it doesn't work to play it safe—and this holds for routine problems as well as Rogue Waves. When leaders edit their feelings, they surrender the source of their strength as human beings.

The Dutch researchers asked the right question:

Leaders must often align employees' behavior with goals that require frequent adaptation to volatile, changing environments, or find they need to communicate multiple and diverse goals within a relatively short span of time. How can leaders accomplish this?[25]

Their research employed videos of leaders' speeches followed by performance tasks. The speeches were manipulated to convey specific emotions, while tasks involving memory, word completion, writing, and proofreading were scored for accuracy. What did they find?

They confirmed that emotions cannot be overridden or tucked away, whether or not the leader is comfortable in expressing them. Leaders' feelings influence their followers more than their words, *and* feelings do it faster. Emotions provide a focus for whatever a leader might be saying to determine if the leader's pronouncements fit the situation or the intended goal. Emotions are a test of leaders' credibility.

Fit is the key to understanding whether an emotional display is helping or hurting the leader's message, and if "buy-in" is being achieved. The ideal fit is one in which feelings, the expression of those feelings, the enacted values, and the leader's desired end-state are tightly aligned.

We were not there with Denise Hudson during her five-hour staff meeting. She told us that she resonated with the workers' sense of frustration. No doubt her team registered her feelings because they were consonant with how they felt and with the realities they faced. Denise's espoused values—"You've got to involve the people . . . and they've got to feel they can tell you they think you're stupid"—were on display when she agreed to be called to account by her staff. Her desired end-state was well served. She wanted to find solutions that would save the plant, and she wanted everyone on board in the quest for those solutions.

Self-awareness and conscious choice about emotional display *is* achievable by leaders. In situations begging for *promotion*—hopes, wishes, and aspirations for a better day to come—leaders can be genuinely upbeat and enthusiastic and create an appealing and attractive vision. They can inspire creativity and risk-taking. But in cases where they need to emphasize *prevention*—duties, obligations, and responsibilities—it is helpful to display authentic worry and concern.

The researchers determined that "leaders can enhance their success by using their emotions to arouse the right motivational mindset in followers."[26] And incidentally, according to their study, the effects of expressive behaviors such as eye contact, verbal fluency, facial expressions, and dynamic gestures are inconclusive. This is good news for leaders who aren't inclined to be theatrical performers, as well as an important correction for followers who over-interpret every move a leader makes. Leaders don't need to be actors.

Be comfortable being you!

Pay heed to the congruence of feelings and your message. Your emotions can be your closest friends, your deepest allies, and your wisest mentors.

Be Full of Hope

When we climb up to the crow's nest (or go up to the balcony in Ron Heifetz and Marty Linsky's metaphor for how to get perspective[27]), we see a pattern in our interviews. Almost without exception, the leaders we interviewed communicated hope—either implicitly through expression and tone of voice or explicitly through their narrative.

A multinational panel of experts assembled to provide established wisdom on what to do in the throes of disaster and mass violence identified *hope* as one of five "empirically supported intervention principles." (The other four are *safety, calming, efficacy,* and *connectedness.*) Two of the specific recommendations concerning hope are "provide services to individuals that help them get their lives back in place" and employ therapy that "identifies, amplifies, and concentrates on building strengths."[28]

"People flourish when they feel hope in their neighborhood and in their bones,"[29] according to the anthropologist Lionel Tiger. Helpful Help requires leaders to be "purveyors of hope," to use a phrase credited to Napoleon Bonaparte.

Barbara Perry and Harry defined hope as "an act that generates movement toward a shared desirable future."[30] In their book, *Putting Hope to Work*, they defined five principles to activate hope as an organizational resource.[31] Renae Conley referred to each of these principles in her Katrina story:

- There is the principle of *possibility*—finding the right level of challenge in a situation as well as having multiple solutions to problems. Renae mentioned "lots of different dimensions of what you're trying to put together to keep moving forward."
- A second principle is *agency*—feeling capable of addressing the tasks at hand and being willing to take them on. Renae's exhortation was "Here's what we have to do today."
- The principle of *worth*—meaningfulness and value—was inherent in Renae's rejection of "stuff." Her question was "How do you want your life to go?"
- The principle of *openness* is trusting fate (or the process) and being curious, not closed-minded, about what could happen. Renae disclosed: "I'm a very spiritual person . . . you come out the other side of it."

- And the hopeful principle of *connection*, which is being both grounded in reality and related to others, was given voice in her desire to help people maintain normality in the midst of chaos.

Hope is the right blend of optimism and realism—a dependable balance for leaders—and is never one-sidedly positive. New research suggests that valiant efforts to stay upbeat and envision a sunny future actually have an opposite effect. They sap focus and energy and get in the way of progress. Psychologist Gabriele Oettingen reports that happy thoughts can be soporific—you feel better but you have less energy. Dwelling on the downsides, however, doesn't work well either. It's most effective to entertain reasonable wishes and explore obstacles in the way. The result is higher mood and energy, plus more flexibility to try something else if the plan isn't working.[32]

Hope is *not* related to overconfidence—being too sure you know the truth. Edward Russo and Paul Shoemaker studied managerial decision traps and concluded: "Be aware when you are functioning as a decider and when your primary role is that of a doer, motivator, or implementer."[33] As with emotional display, take heed of what you feel and think and what you're trying to accomplish. When deciding, be realistic. When implementing, be confident. Awareness and perspective are paramount. Find your personal crow's nest and look down on the waves, the boat, your crew, and yourself.

The Roundhouse of Helpful Help

Courtney Wilson is director of the B&O Railroad Museum in Baltimore, the finest collection of historic railway artifacts in the country.[34] The circular 1884 building, designed by a noted B&O architect, has 22 sides and stands 123 feet high. In 2003, the roof of the museum's roundhouse collapsed under the weight of two feet of snow, causing damage to beloved railway antiques and threatening the life of the museum itself.

It was devastating news in the global rail-fan community. The pain was organizational and it was personal. Courtney, like other leaders mentioned in these pages, struggled to manage his public emotional response to the disaster:

I cried a tremendous amount, but no one ever saw me do it. I had to find those private places to go to get my emotions out. I knew I couldn't let anyone see me break. Believe me, that's exhausting. You can't even let anyone see your lip tremble. And that takes a lot of energy.

As it happened, Courtney was scheduled to deliver a keynote address at a conference of museum directors two days after the roof collapsed.

He prepared the speech he thought he was supposed to give for the occasion. But once he stepped up to the podium he set it aside and spoke directly about what he knew and what he felt in the wake of the fiasco. His raw passion merged with authoritative descriptions of wrecked rolling stock. He blended heart and head.

Courtney led the renovation of the museum. And he continued to speak out, finding a broader stage for his message. Many have wanted to hear how to cope in an emergency. He's shared his story more than 250 times with professional groups.

> *I call it "Managing Reaction." I've given that "dog and pony show" all across the US to both corporate and nonprofit folks because what I discovered is, I don't care how many disaster plans you have written or walked through, other than giving you basic information or contact information for outside help, most of those plans tend to get tossed in the circular file. Whatever you're dealing with isn't described in there.*
>
> *Planning is good. I think it teaches leaders to think critically to gather resources. And I think something disaster plans never address is . . . managing reaction.*
>
> *But let's take that down to a personal level. There's no disaster plan that teaches you how to manage the emotions of an institution's constituents or its employees. In the case of a nonprofit (like us) we have a broad constituent base of people (for whom) the loss of something like this would have been disastrous.*

Courtney is now advising other nonprofit institutions facing closure. He's reimagined himself as a leader. His beneficiaries include his Roundhouse, other museums, students who have learned from his published case study, and leaders who have heard him speak. What goes around comes around. Courtney's version of Helpful Help has circled back and helped him too.

> *I had to learn to walk blindly by adapting my external face to the world, to not produce a "woe is me" or "we have a lot of work to do" or "I'm ignoring you" (external face), but to really be a spokesperson for the fact that, we were confident, we were trusting in our ability to garner the resources to survive this.*
>
> *I turned my personal ship around . . . to reassure people that everything was going to be okay.*
>
> *On a very personal level, I had to do that with my employees as well. I remember the morning after the first reports of the roof collapse. We were all snowed in at home, except me. Our employees were devastated, but one of their major concerns was, "Do I have a job?" My answer was an unrepentant "Absolutely! You have a job!" Not knowing where the money would be coming from to continue to pay them, I knew that was the right answer, what they needed to hear . . . .*

I think if you asked me what the greatest transformation (that) occurred in me was, it was really learning that the emotional response to any kind of Rogue Wave can in many instances be a critical factor in whether you're going to be successful in surviving or not.

People need to know that you're a human being, and that you're hurting. But they need to continue to know that you have it under control, and that they can continue to trust the decisions you make.

In the immediate aftermath of the collapse, Courtney told a reporter,

As a leader, it was my job to offer a positive attitude, even though I was wondering, "Would the museum survive?" Notes, letters, emails, and contributions literally came in from around the world. It was then I realized we're going to make it.[35]

In fact they did make it. Helpful Help was delivered, received, and echoed in a circle of support that existed far beyond the Roundhouse.

Helpful Help is an outward reach provoked by an inward turn. Its source is in knowing ourselves very well and in being mindful of our actions. Ram Dass and Paul Gorman ask, "*Will we look within?* Can we see that to be of most service to others we must face our own doubts, needs, and resistance? We've never grown without having done so."[36] They say, "Compassion for ourselves, perspective, humor . . . these are our allies."[37] We get perspective, find humor, and experience self-compassion when we help others. It is a powerful cycle of strength for the organization and the leader.

Everyone benefits from your being there with others, listening, being in touch with what you feel, and enacting hope. Indeed, *everyone* would benefit if *everyone* followed your lead as Helpful Helper.

5

It Was a Dark and Stormy Night: Leadership Storytelling

In the tale, in the telling, we are all one blood.[1]

—Ursula K. Le Guin

We've all heard this story or some variation while sitting under the stars on a summer's evening:

It was a dark and stormy night, and sailors great and small, sat around a campfire, all. Said the captain to the mate, "Mate, tell us a story." And this is the way the story went.

"It was a dark and stormy night, and sailors great and small, sat around a campfire, all. Said the captain to the mate. . . ."

It's a mischievous campfire story about a campfire story that circles on and on. "Dark and Stormy Night" contains the five main elements of storytelling: *storyteller* (the narrator), *listeners* (the sailors around a campfire), the *story* itself (such as it is), its *context* (a blustery night implying chills and fears), and finally, *intent* (amusement at someone else's expense). We gleefully retell the story every chance we get.

Storytelling in the wake of a Rogue Wave is anything but a joke. The *storyteller* (crisis leader) tells a *story* that pulls the organization into a circle of *listeners*. The crisis provides riveting *context*. The *intent* is to help the community heal. When leaders use storytelling effectively, the community is given a chance to recover from today and turn to the future.

One of our core messages for leaders in times of disaster is to *embrace the function of storytelling*. Don't delegate it to your mate—your communications department, press secretary, deputy assistant, HR professional, or any other stand-in. When your community has been wounded, it's up to you to lead, and that means telling the story.

As a Rogue Wave leader, you become Storyteller-in-Chief.

Howard Gardner, the Harvard developmental psychologist best known for the theory of multiple intelligences, having examined the minds of a selection of world leaders, concluded: "A key—perhaps *the* [emphasis his] key—to leadership, as well as to the garnering of a following, is the effective communication of a story."[2] Eleanor Roosevelt, Alfred P. Sloan, and Mahatma Gandhi, among others, provide his examples. For four decades, Roosevelt told and retold chapters in her life's story framed as an ordinary person who could overcome obstacles (in books, articles, and a newspaper column) and became the most influential woman of her time. Sloan communicated the greatness of General Motors as an institution serving the public interest by expressing and exhibiting his personal belief in enterprise and progress. Gandhi embodied his story of spiritual power and stuck with it, changing the course of India.

Storytelling has gained so many adherents among today's leaders and their educators that it is now considered a core leadership competency.[3] It's a learnable skill and the best way to communicate complex messages. Stories motivate people and help everyone move in the same direction. Stories connect people to larger purposes as well as with each other. Stories are remembered and shared.

When people retell stories, they enact ancestral traditions of oral transmission and collective meaning making. Storytelling reminds us of the iconic campfire around which we gather to hear the same message and further our sense of being connected. And for organizations focused on results and the bottom line, stories trigger gains in employee engagement—the holy grail of organizational performance.[4]

If story is vital to community, it is indispensable to a community in crisis.

Story can restore order, and storytelling leaders can regain organizational trust. Remember, leaders are being *blamed* for events they didn't cause or see coming. The organization is within its rights to expect coherent leadership at such a time. If you are the leader, your story, your storytelling, and you as a person are joined in a decisive moment.

A leader who can *author* a story for the organization is securing a special kind of *authority*, the power of engaging people and providing direction. In this chapter we explore what it means to be a leader who uses the power of storytelling in a crisis as author, authority, and Storyteller-in-Chief. We begin with a focus on the power of story, to *restore*, which is why it all matters.

Story Restores

When we interviewed leaders and asked about Rogue Waves, everyone had a tale to tell about being deeply shaken by an event that was not supposed to happen or happen that way. Each person recalled at least one painful moment of shock, fright, and confusion.

When Frank Kaminski, an Illinois police chief, heard about a child abducted by a bad guy, it was a calamity for his small, quiet town. For Frank, "The world changed. Everything was upside down."[5]

When Rose Ott was fired for whistle-blowing at the investment company where she held a senior position, she was so taken down by the behavior of her former colleagues she "had to recreate herself."[6]

Dean Scarborough, CEO of Avery Dennison, realized after the market crash of 2008 that the company was so "incredibly vulnerable" he had to compartmentalize his feelings in order to function.[7]

In a rare public statement, U.S. Airways CEO Doug Parker admitted to the press that when he learned (at 6: 43 am, on August 13, 2013, a date burned into memory) that the Department of Justice was suing on antitrust grounds to stop the merger with American Airlines, he was bowled over. "Business people aren't supposed to be surprised, but we were absolutely surprised."[8]

Tom Yeomans, a spiritual psychologist, was once "blindsided" by colleagues during a painful rift. He was painfully made aware of what he called a "huge blind spot about peoples' dark sides" that was all the more distressing because of his experience and role.[9] "I couldn't see it—it was an encounter with a dark force, and I had to learn more about myself in order to be more helpful to others. It changed my career."

In a crisis, we lose our sense of direction, emotionally, spiritually, and practically. Our expected relationships can't be trusted. Rogue Waves threaten meaning, "the expected relationships or associations connecting people, places, objects and beliefs to each other."[10]

Meaning is essential to survival because it "allows us to feel like we understand our experiences."[11] Without it, we're not sure we know what's going on, or why, or what might happen next. We can't see patterns or make connections. We're baffled, bewildered, and staggered. Without meaning, we're not fully human.

Viktor Frankl, having survived Auschwitz, concluded: "Woe to him who saw no more sense in his life, no aim, no purpose, and therefore no point in carrying on. He was soon lost."[12]

Rogue Waves splinter our lives' *stories.*

When meaning is violated, we feel a "special kind of bad."[13] Psychologists call this feeling aversive arousal, or dissonance, or disequilibrium. When there's a gap between what we've been taking for granted and what has just shown up, we want to close that gap, and fast. Deep contradictions are hard for us to live with.

For Ronnie Janoff-Bulman, a psychology professor, we maintain three fundamental assumptions to help us feel safe: The world is meaningful. The world is benevolent. The self is worthy.[14] She writes that our internal dialogue goes something like this:

> *My world is benevolent. Even in such a good world negative things happen, even if relatively infrequently. Yet when they occur they are not random, but rather are meaningfully distributed. They happen to people who deserve them, either because of who they are or what they did or failed to do. I am a good, competent, careful person. Bad things couldn't happen to me.*[15]

A meaningful world doesn't allow random bad things to happen, and a benevolent world delivers the bad only when it's deserved. But a Rogue Wave delivers unexpected and unmerited harm. Does that mean we are absolved of responsibility? Should we do penance for bad things if we didn't cause them?

Barry Dym suggests not. Self-laceration after a Rogue Wave is based on a "perverse idea of being in control."[16] We have difficulty dealing with the idea that the world is impersonal. We want to see ourselves as being *agentic*—we want to feel we can make things happen. So when awful stuff happens of its own accord, it's a double whammy. Not only are fundamental beliefs cast in doubt, but our self-confidence is also diminished. It's more than a setback, and much more than egg on our face. The psychic injury can be deep, we are suddenly changed, and we will never forget.

Psychologically, we engage in any number of behaviors to restore the familiar and reduce the pain of having our mental models shattered. What psychologists call the "meaning maintenance model" says we will do whatever we can to self-soothe:

- Where there is a disruption in the validity of our beliefs,
- When we sense loss of control,

- When we feel we no longer belong where we are, or
- When we are reminded of our own mortality, which is the most threatening of all.

In these circumstances we gather up our egos and run toward whatever we think is normal or constant or predictable.[17]

We may tell ourselves that some larger purpose is being served or that life just happens. How else can we come to grips?

Any one of a number of psychological defenses is always at our disposal. Some, like humor and altruism, are more mature than others like escapism or denial, which are primitive.[18] Taking a mental holiday and fantasizing about being on a fair-weather day in a tropical sea obviously would not have been a mature choice for Kyle Garcia.

If we are creative, we may express our feelings through poetry, music, art, or dance. There's no single psychological theory that captures all the ways we try to cope with Rogue Waves. Yet we believe there is a positive and pragmatic principle of leadership that works for self and others in the darkest hour. When the sea engulfs a lighthouse, sailors' coordinates are obscured. When events overwhelm an organization, people lose their touch points. *Story* restores meaning and shores up leaders. It also restores the organization.

An Identity Story

Ronnie Janoff-Bulman quotes one of her mentors, the late Philip Brickman: "Though not the master of one's fate, one may still be captain of one's own soul."[19] Wisdom is rooted in understanding this distinction and acting accordingly. When we hold leaders accountable for outcomes over which they have little control, we commit a fundamental attribution error. Yet leaders *are* responsible for their personal identity, for who they are, and how they lead others.

Chief Russell Laine's story is one of many we heard about a leader who became master of his soul.[20] Russell told his story from the vantage point of retirement, looking back over a long career as police chief in a suburban Chicago town and president of both state and international associations of chiefs of police. We wanted to hear his story.

Russell has been in recovery for twenty years. "Early on in my career, I did a lot of drinking, and that was how I processed things." His story unfolded in the context of battling addiction.

One night, Chief Laine raced to the scene of a suicide after being called at home. A young woman, formerly a dispatcher in his department, had been in a troubled relationship with a man who was once her supervisor on the force. She was at his house when she took his service revolver and killed herself. Chief Laine was devastated.

> There's really nothing that prepares you for something like this. You are emotionally and personally hit. This was a sweet young girl. After the event you start hearing many other stories of threat and suicide and events that occurred between her and the supervisor. How did I miss it?

The small community was in chaos, and "many people's lives were changed as a result of that," said Russell.

> Quite frankly, that was the turning point of my life. I started off with the booze. I couldn't tell you right now how long the drinking continued after that, but I knew I was heading for self-destruction.
>
> I got involved in recovery. I had reached the limits of the booze solution. At that time I could look at everything else in my life and how booze was interfering. I guess in one sense I was fortunate. The suicide became a life-changing event for me. I remember crying in my drink.
>
> I also remember coming sober and thinking about it and processing the tears and the pain. At that point I took ownership of that. This is real pain and it's okay, and I just need to move on. There are things I have to take care of, including myself.

When Russell stopped drinking, many things turned around. He credits God, his wife, a sponsor, his parents, mentors, and other supportive people for his recovery. Russell is a different man today. His father, a hard-working music teacher whom he loved and respected, acknowledged that Russell was "fun to be around again."

He bolstered his sobriety with courage and self-scrutiny.

> You get to the point where you conceivably can lose it, you stop for yourself, and then you go on. You can have those feelings of despair but at that point in time you have a mission you need to accomplish and you need to deal with that.

Russell's new mission was to speak honestly about alcohol and substance abuse *by police officers*. From the vantage of his hard-won sobriety, he knew the score. From his position as president of the International Association of Chiefs of Police, he focused attention on substance abuse among police offices. He began shining light on a problem with which he was very familiar, putting his personal pain and hurt to work for the good of others. His efforts opened the door for new and important conversations that launched initiatives to help police handle stress in better, positive ways. "Sometimes it's planting that seed today that won't grow until the next season or two seasons down the road . . . that might help."

Russell's story is more than a story of his trouble, his crisis, and his rebound. His story has an ancient formulation. It is a leader's journey to a mature identity that leads to restoration for others. He functioned in two spheres at once. Privately, Russell had been stunned if not shattered. Publicly, he had remained the responsible face of the police force and community. Chief Laine's story was simultaneously self-talk and communication with others. Speaking to a crowd, listening to yourself—this parallel tracking is inherent in the leadership job of helping people heal while healing oneself.

Crisis sharpens everyone's senses. Leaders can find solace and power in telling stories. When speaking to a crowd of unsettled, anxious, grieving, or even angry people, the storyteller's courage may be eloquent. When there is deep value in the story, the telling of it can be restorative for all.

Dan McAdams, chair of the Department of Psychology at Northwestern University, explains that we define ourselves by the personal myths and life stories we tell ourselves. For leaders, autobiographical stories are uniquely powerful in their ability to legitimate themselves *as leaders*—as authentic members of the community whom we choose to follow.[21]

Identity stories, the stories leaders tell about themselves, are shortcuts to getting to know them. As we listen for every nuance in word and tone, and watch for expression and gesture, we decide to follow, to reserve judgment, or to run the other way. For McAdams, a fundamental quality is authenticity—"the extent to which his or her actions, words, and identity correspond with each other."[22]

But authenticity is not normative. It doesn't necessarily imply goodness or right behavior or positive ends. A person can be *authentic* and exhibit a certain consistency of character while representing any number of paranoid, negative, or degrading attitudes and behaviors. When core questions such as "What is our shared purpose?" are on the minds of everyone in the organization, they can't be answered by the leader's authenticity alone.

McAdams argues that leadership purpose is closely tied with the ancient human theme of *redemption*: "deliverance from suffering to a better world."[23] In a Rogue Wave, more is required of us because so much is at stake. Leaders must speak the truth in order to maintain trust and believability. They must also *represent* how something good can be born out of the bad—this is derived from their stories of redemption.

When leaders narrate their journey of redemption, from pain to Promised Land, people will follow. Leaders who share such stories personify a powerful, redeeming spirit. They lead by personal example. They don't cheerlead. They bear witness to possibilities for recovery and renewal. And as they author their stories, they deepen and extend their leadership mark. Yet leaders' stories do not need to be epochal to be redemptive. They need to be real, and they need to advocate a positive view of human progress: *how to make a difference in peoples' lives and make the world a better place.*

An Organizational Story

The story of another police chief, again told without bravado, conveys the theme of redemption, with a direct line to organizational improvement. George Graves, former marine, veteran police officer, and a Catholic, told us about stubbornness in the face of discrimination.[24]

Chief Graves was chief of police in a suburban Chicago village that he described the town as "a WASP community, where the power base comes out of a particular Protestant church there, and where Catholics are discriminated against."

One day, his newly elected village president came to see him and said, "People on the street tell me I should fire you."

George asked, "What's it all about?"

"Well," said the town official, "I'll come back in two weeks and talk to you." George felt the guy wanted him "to sit and stew on it."

The president came back in two weeks and reported that there was really just one person who had a problem. But, he warned, "the man's roots go down to the core of the earth in this community." It turned out that this was a local businessman who owned and operated nine trucks and didn't want to buy stickers to register his vehicles. The president wanted George to have the accrued tickets discharged without payment.

"I say, 'I never interfere with arrests,' said George. And he says, 'Oh, yes, you will.' "

George didn't.

The scofflaw businessman eventually went to court, lost the suit, got fined, and was required to buy the licenses for his vehicles. But the story didn't end there.

The village president commissioned an audit of the police department. As it happened, the audit turned out to be very favorable. When it was all over, the consultant who had performed the audit revealed that he had been instructed to find dirt on George. "George Graves is a Catholic. There have got to be worms under the rock. Find the worms."

Anti-Catholic harassment of this sort continued for the four years of the president's term. The truth is that such sentiment was deep-seated in the town.

George was supported by his troops, who were watching from the sidelines wondering, "How is the Old Man going to deal with this?" The ruckus was having an effect on them, too. His department was half-Protestant, half other faiths. For George,

> *It increased my resolve. I'm a good cop and also a good leader and a good administrator, and I'm stubborn . . . I figured if I continued to adhere to ethical principles and provide good services I could rely on the fact that people would recognize it.*

What George lived through increased his empathy for others in similar predicaments. "When I interact with minorities or people who have little voice, I have an understanding where they are coming from."

Chief Graves finished his career as police chief in another town, one where his department became only the second in the state to be reviewed and accredited by a national commission. At the close of the accreditation hearing, with his mayor and managers present, the commission chairman said,

> *I have one more comment for you, Chief. I noticed when looking at the demographics of the town that you're not a very diverse community. But yet your department is diverse, and I compliment you.*

For George, it was a proud moment. "We were just looking for the best people, and we had some Hispanics, we had some Blacks, some Asians who made it." He quipped, "It wasn't really purposeful on our part but we took the credit for it anyway." He took credit, if obliquely, by relating a lesson learned at the FBI National Academy that the person at the top sets the tone for the organization.

The crisis and political pressure George experienced were a test of his authenticity. They sowed the seeds for his performance as an inclusive leader. Out of crisis came a leader's story of redemption. His police force and community were the beneficiaries.

Neither Chief Laine nor Chief Graves would describe themselves as storytellers. Yet they narrated *authentic stories of redemption* that extended their leadership in powerful ways. Neither sought the limelight nor construed storytelling as entertainment. Chief Laine gave speeches and Chief Graves made quiet decisions. Each addressed social issues—substance abuse and religious discrimination—by naming and facing them, and then putting the storylines to use.

When leaders tell stories born of crisis they have personally experienced, they restore organizations.

The Power of Story

Some leaders we interviewed were stirred by the power of their stories. Some choked up. Some shut down. Others thanked us because, "It was good for me to talk." Too many, we observed, have not told their stories at all or they've tucked them away and not revisited them in a long while. Too few recalled telling their stories with an appreciation of how their stories could help other people. They related how they had changed for the better, and they gave evidence of real accomplishments for the common good. They acknowledged beneficial lessons, yet they had not put their stories to use.

Meaning does not appear in nicely wrapped packages. How do you make meaning when you're facing chaos? There's no manual that explains the stages involved. There are no preordained steps for the personal journey that will hone deep insight. "Meaning is not something out there that is given to us; it is something we give to ourselves," writes Stephen Joseph. "We do that through stories."[25]

The function of a story in a Rogue Wave is to make mindboggling events comprehensible. The storytelling leader has a duty to make sense of events as a voice of reason, hope, and meaning. Some leaders employed story in remarkable fashion, going beyond recovery to personal and organizational rejuvenation. Yet for others, storytelling in a crisis is not an obvious move. For them, the solutions are detailed in emergency manuals and dictated by predetermined procedures and not revealed in stories.

Most leaders can communicate with overt messages and careful, fact-based arguments. Some leaders will hesitate in going beyond any utterance that is completely, literally correct. Many have been technically trained in science and engineering, finance and accounting, law, or information technology. They have risen through the ranks by virtue of their ability to know specifics, to find out details, or to argue fine points. For them, truth is accuracy. Sometimes they resist going off script even though the task is to reassure, inspire, or describe something that sits out of rational reach.

In times of turbulence precise accuracy in communications is mostly out of reach. Karl Weick says that in a situation such as a Rogue Wave, when events are unfolding quickly, when there are multiple possible meanings intended for multiple audiences, and when reliable information is minimal, leaders still need to react with dispatch. As if to reassure, Weick says accuracy may be "nice but not necessary."

What *is* necessary is to make some sort of sense in the situation with

> [s]omething that preserves plausibility and coherence, something that is reasonable and memorable, something that embodies past experience and expectations, something which resonates with other people, something that can be constructed retrospectively but also can be used prospectively, something that captures both feeling and thought, something that allows for embellishment to fit current oddities, something that is fun to contrast. In short, what is necessary in sensemaking is a good story.[26]

If leaders take the leap and deviate from carefully choreographed performances using graphs and charts, and tell stories, how does it work?

Melanie Green, a social psychologist, describes the process of being influenced by story as "transportation into a narrative world." She doesn't mean something magical. Instead, this is the everyday experience of being lost in a story whether spoken, read, or acted. Green is referring to our *emotional* response. "A transported individual is fully mentally engaged with the story, responds emotionally to it, and may experience vivid mental images of story events."[27]

It doesn't seem to matter whether the story is told as fact or fiction. We *read into* the stories we are told, and we create potential realities. We claim the meaning as ours. This happens at home as our children soak up our family stories. And this happens at work when we tell stories about how it used to be around here.

Green's theory explains that when stories work really well they change beliefs in three ways. First, the listening space created by stories reduces resistance. The normal "yes, but" reaction from listeners who expect concrete and specific answers is suspended. Second, because listeners feel like participants in unfolding events, they feel personally addressed. Learning seems more about them. Third, when feelings evoked by stories are related to love (caring, compassion, and concern), listeners will more readily identify with the characters in the story as well as the storyteller and take to heart the story's lessons and intent.

When stories resonate, the "universal singular" is at work. According to Norman Denzin, a communications scholar at the University of Illinois, each of us relates to the storyteller personally—as if hearing a story as being just about *me*—while at the same time being aware that the story is *not* about me at all. As Denzin says, "Every person is like every other person, but like no other person."[28]

Stories are uniquely well suited to changing attitudes. Green examined how narrative messages, versus arguments and rhetoric, affected individual responses to loaded issues such as affirmative action and homosexuality. She and her colleagues discovered that empathic feelings evoked through story changed beliefs. Logic and reason were not persuasive. Green concludes that stories appeared to change the gut feelings lying beneath deeply held social views.[29]

According to the storyteller Hannah Harvey, stories serve multiple functions such as establishing the identity of and membership in a group, making life coherent while questioning what is happening in the moment, and revealing human truths.[30] This can be of huge value in a crisis. People need gut-checks not spreadsheets. Why would we expect people to be soothed by rational analysis when the world has become absurd?

New research indicates that stories play out very differently than facts. How a leader communicates influences both whether the message is received and the degree to which the leader is well perceived. In several experiments conducted by researchers at the University of North Carolina, participants read vignettes of advice-giving conversations online and judged the speakers according to their competence and warmth.[31] When the topic being discussed required facts, such as which bank offered the best mortgage rate, the speaker who presented statistics was judged more competent than a second speaker who spoke of the experience of dealing with the same bank. The second speaker scored points for being warm, but not for being competent.

But when the topic shifted and required more than just facts and figures—in this case, travel—results were different. The statistical argument ("travellers' ratings are high") failed to garner its speaker more credibility, while the narrative approach ("my friend went there and had a wonderful time") was warmly received. Travel invites a much broader array of issues than finding a mortgage, and an organizational crisis is much more difficult to talk about than a numbers-based profit target.

The leader who dances around tough issues and offers vague generalities in the face of a storm will no doubt lose credibility. But when issues are complex, warmth matters as much as numbers. "Facts are friendly" is a reliable management credo. And so are stories.

Stories that pack a wallop, such as the hero's journey from ordeal to triumph, resonate because they shift our emotions from suspense to excitement to fear to relief. The emotional journey hooks. We want to reexperience it, do some research and find out more about it, or share the experience with our friends. In fact, the more intense the emotional experience, the more we want to share it, and the more it goes viral. When a leader tells a story and discloses emotion, it "spreads not simply the emotion but the information it generated to others."[32]

In an emotionally charged event—think Rogue Wave—people want to share. They seek an outlet, a way to release the powerful emotions they are experiencing together. Leadership in these moments means finding ways to achieve organizational catharsis while imparting information needed for survival. These go hand-in-glove. It is in everyone's best interest that gripping stories are told by leaders, in the crux of the moment, in order to provoke social sharing of feelings and facts.

In the 1990s, Louis Gerstner was hired to rescue IBM from bankruptcy. He started out among the anti-vision-thing crowd. "The last thing IBM needs now is a vision: it needs lower costs and better market focus in every division." Howard Gardner observes how Gerstner soon changed his tune. "You've got to appeal to people's emotions," recanted Gerstner. "They've got to buy in with their hearts and their beliefs, not just their minds." So Gerstner soon had a new story, and that story helped him succeed.[33]

Organizational coherence relies on members knowing where the enterprise came from, what it does, and how well and what purpose it serves. In routine times, coherence targeted at a desired end is considered strategy. Charts and graphs, numbers and logic play important roles. But during calamities, coherence becomes even more vital. It can be essential to survival. Posting data, sending updates, and sharing the latest news are necessary, but not sufficient. Stressed and frightened people cannot be enlisted with carefully constructed, factual explanations. They can only be reminded of the deep reasons for their common endeavor, through story. People want more than a weather report.

We are *not* talking about war stories. Many of us discount the power of storytelling in organizations because we remember awkward moments when speakers went off subject in an attempt to present themselves in a favorable light or to dodge an unwelcome truth. Perhaps they simply wanted to share an amazing adventure. Or they believed they were telling a story that had a lesson or a point, though it wasn't made clear to the audience. No matter the reason, crisis storytelling that comes across as being primarily for the benefit of the storyteller is inept, or worse.

Leadership stories are told for *the benefit of the organization*.

When an organization's identity is endangered, associates long to hear shared stories refreshed and retold. Tales about how they have overcome challenges and found victory in the past become much more than fun reminiscences. According to Paul Zak, a neuroeconomist at Claremont College, "These are the stories that, repeated over and over, stay core to the organization's DNA. They provide guidance for daily decision-making as well as the motivation that comes with the conviction that the organization's work must go on, and needs everyone's full engagement to make a difference in people's lives."[34]

Zak, author of *The Moral Molecule: The Source of Love and Prosperity*, researches the role of oxytocin, a neurochemical in the brain he says allows us to know whom to trust. He's discovered that if you develop *tension* in the story, you'll sustain attention and release oxytocin. If you tell the Rogue Wave story and share your emotions, your listeners are likely to mimic the feelings and behaviors of the story's characters, thus motivating cooperation and empathy.[35] "To the brain, good stories are good stories, whether first-person or third-person, on topics happy or sad, as long as they get us to care about their characters."[36]

Some caution is in order. Herminia Ibarra of the Harvard Business School warns that our stories can become outdated. Just as with proverbial war stories, stories can outlive their validity or their usefulness. We should not feel compelled to stick to them, come what may. Instead, we should edit them as we do our resumes, and tell them in a new light.[37] We are free to change or reinterpret our stories as we retell them, just as others will do as they pass them on. Only by being flexible and newly creative can we remain evergreen.

One more caution: Jonathan Gottschall, who teaches English at Washington and Jefferson College, writes, "Humans evolved to crave a story."[38] Stories are powerful, so handle with care. We may be susceptible to self-amusement and be enamored with our ability to entertain. When your inner storyteller hijacks you and you get carried away, be on the alert. Your favorite example, anecdote, or theory may not serve your larger purpose. Keep your inner editor plugged in.

We recognize several paradoxical communications questions that challenge leaders, especially in a crisis. Storytelling is not a ready-fire activity. Impact may require forethought and practice. For example, how do you send messages that touch every listener, while strengthening their group identity? How do you give directions that are nonnegotiable, while empowering people to buy in and take those directions to heart? How do you speak in concrete terms about what is happening or needs to happen next, as you appeal to abstract values and principles? These and other puzzles confront leaders as they go before their followers in highly charged moments of uncertainty.

For us, there's no better way to communicate complexity, ambiguity, and paradox than with story. A crisis heightens the importance of Storyteller-in-Chief.

Storyteller-in-Chief

When bombs exploded near the finish line of the 2013 Boston Marathon, the world was horrified. When the suspects were identified as Muslims three days later, the Islamic community of Boston felt a second wave of anguish. The media were amplifying a negative narrative about Muslims. How should U.S. citizens living in New England who are also Muslims respond?

Soon after the bombing in Boston, it was uncovered that one of the suspected bombers had attended the Cambridge Mosque, across the river. This relatively small mosque was suddenly at the center of media attention, and yet it lacked anyone to handle the press. The greater Muslim community in the city knew they needed to respond. "We made the calculation that we needed to defend the Cambridge Mosque because, either way, the name of the Boston Muslim community would be hurt if there was no one to clarify what we were about," said Yusufi Vali, who was soon tapped by elders to be their spokesperson.[39]

Yusufi was the recently appointed executive director of the 1,300-member Islamic Center of Boston. He grew up a Midwestern Muslim in Lee's Summit, Missouri, having emigrated from Nagpur, India, when he was nine years old. His father had been an accomplished engineer in India, but at first he could only find a temporary job in the United States distributing Yellow Page directories. After three years, his dad found permanent work as a wastewater treatment engineer, and the family celebrated at a Pizza Hut, a favorite local restaurant. At that moment, Yusufi's "American dream was truly born."

Yusufi played sports and developed his faith—"not once" feeling anti-Muslim discrimination. He became a star soccer player and was valedictorian of his class, and he was the first person in his school to be accepted at Princeton.[40]

Later a Marshall Scholar who studied in England, Yusufi felt called to go to Boston and do purposeful work in support of his religious community. He had risen quickly within the Islamic Center, but when he was asked to be spokesperson for the Cambridge Mosque in the heat of the crisis, he was faced with an enormous challenge and he was consumed with self-doubt. He felt unprepared to be the voice of the community.

And why should he have to do this anyway, he asked himself?

Frankly, we could not consider them (the accused bombers) part of our faith community. We didn't have anything to do with them. These guys didn't come to my cultural center.

Yusufi struggled to come to terms with it all. "Why am I being asked to do this, to be the face of public relations? What would this mean for my career or my family?" Meanwhile, the media frenzy was heating up. To find his way, he said a "combo" of things helped: praying, being reassured by his wife, taking advice from close friends, consulting with media experts, and receiving the perspective of a wise board member:

God is calling you to take this on. You have the potential to take this on. You will get a lot of blessings for taking this on.

Yusufi was confused and scared, yet he was buoyed by the confidence his spiritual advisors had in him. He took to heart their message, "You can do this. It's a reminder of why you got into this in the first place." In an "alone moment," Yusufi "had a conversation with himself" and became clear about what he should do. He remembered his much larger purpose.

I was trying to serve God. God had called me to this position. The realization that God wouldn't have made this happen if God didn't think I could deal with this. And God wanted me to go through this training.

Now he was ready: "I knew that I had to make this decision and really own being the spokesperson."

Unprepared by experience and training, and never before having been the one in the hot seat, Yusufi stepped up to the microphone and spoke to the world of his community's grief, solidarity, and deep loyalty to Boston. It was a true crisis moment when story and leadership merged. Yusufi exercised courage, handled the media, and gave voice to reason and perspective. It was on-the-job training, and Yusufi was a quick study.

Previously, Yusufi's work had been about building a faith community. Now his work was to build a larger community of citizens and neighbors. But the most profound thing Yusufi learned was how the Muslim is perceived in the public sphere.

A liberal journalist would call me but would not ask, "Did someone in your congregation get hurt? Is there a hero in your congregation?" Instead, the question was, "How is the backlash? Is everything OK?"—which means they perceive us as victims. Then a right wing journalist would ask, "Did these guys come to your Mosque?"—insinuating that we were connected. So they saw us as perpetrators. But no one would see us as part of the city. That was the challenge: How do we get people to understand that we are part of the city?

Yusufi realized he had once been comfortable speaking as an "other" and playing into stereotypes of weakness and pity. Now he felt the narrative had to change. He was no longer willing to allow the Boston Muslim community to "other" themselves and be distanced from society. He rose above his insecurities to be true to his beliefs. He told a story of citizenry solidarity.

When I speak publicly now I think very carefully about how to speak about being a Bostonian, and not as the Muslim "other."

Yusufi Vali emerged from his Rogue Wave wiser, tougher, a leader—and a storyteller. He found his voice and shaped a new agenda. He communicated collective hurt while speaking deeply of his personal shock and dismay. He changed his life and philosophy while making a difference in the lives of others.

Yusufi's storytelling bears witness to the efficacy of a powerful story and the significance of how it is told. He graduated to a role we call Storyteller-in-Chief, a leader who understands and employs storytelling. And he accomplished this inside a Rogue Wave.

The role of Storyteller-in Chief is central to our thinking about narrating an organizational crisis. How does it work?

Professional storytellers think in terms of a central storytelling triangle to explain the relationship among story, teller, and audience. They are aware how storytelling is not one-way communication of information to listeners. Instead, storytelling is a relationship in which each element influences and is influenced by the others. "At its best, storytelling is a dynamic dialogue—one in which the teller listens to what the audience needs, the audience listens to the story and the teller, and the story moves back and forth between them."[41]

A Storyteller-in-Chief is embedded, as illustrated in the following display, in a nest of sources. Storytellers must pull their personal experience into the story and be cognizant of how they have been affected by crisis. That's how they put their skin in the game, and that's what makes them real.

At the same time they must be aware of the experiences suffered by the organization as well as their audiences' needs in that very moment. That's what grounds them and makes their story credible.

The situation can be likened to William James's description of a baby's first experience of the world as "one great blooming, buzzing confusion."[42] Unlike what it means for an infant, Rogue Wave confusion has immediate and significant consequences for many other people. Storytelling is *not* aimed at light-hearted diversion, innocent fellowship, or reminiscence of times past. The sought-for solution is a specific outcome—shared meaning. New stories are needed.

In Figure 5.1, shared meaning is shown to be *communally* created, as indicated by its connection to the leader's story and the organizational audience. The leader doesn't *formulate* it and then *share*. Success is not indicated by whether there is buy-in with the leader's point of view. Instead, the story comes alive when it's heard and retold, pulling everyone into a common frame while encouraging each person to take it home and make it personal.

Lani Peterson, a noted storyteller, explains that a good story must have a *storyline* and an arc—a path from beginning to end that captures the imagination of listeners and carries them along. "The arc is not complete until there is a going-back to the beginning in a new way to make a difference in other people's lives. It's not just what you do, it's what you do for others that matters."[43] Yusufi's story has a powerful storyline at the heart of his telling. The storyline arc is a U-shaped curve extending down and then back up. Powerful stories like Yusufi's begin with a threat, a setback, or a challenge. Then there is a reversal of some sort, a sudden turn of events that is unexpected and unwelcome.

Yusufi's story begins with not one but two reversals. The first reversal was a Rogue Wave for everyone, the Boston Marathon bombings. For Yusufi that was a break—a chasm, really—in his quintessential American success story. What followed was a second descending turn, felt acutely in the Muslim community in Massachusetts, and that was the media firestorm.

The word for this beginning-with-reversal is *peripety*—the downward slope of the story's arc.[44] Yusufi told us about the dark times in the days that followed. His sensitivity to the context of prejudice, violence, and hysteria demanded serious soul-searching. He struggled with his identity and role.

Then the direction of the story turned. Bolstered by faith and what we call Helpful Help, Yusufi stepped forward. The story's arc curved upward. Yusufi changed the nature of his internal narrative and influenced the

Leadership Storytelling

Figure 5.1

public conversation. He grew as a leader, and the larger community grew in understanding of the issues at stake. This is how the story was resolved.

Note how the arc has an expected *sequence* as well, as the storyline proceeds left to right corresponding to the passage of time. Commonly, there is an order of events that begins at peripety and proceeds to resolution, not like a complex novel with flashbacks and foreshadows.

When coaching leaders, we sometimes ask them to start at the beginning and take us through it. Yusufi's story began with the bombings. He was asked to play a new role. He sweated the decision but stepped up and succeeded as spokesperson and community leader.

Even though the storyline might be clear, it takes a storytelling leader to bring it to life. A story needs a narrator.[45] Yusufi said, in effect, "I was called to respond to events which I did, and this is how I see them." We hear him as the central actor in the story.

Yusufi told us a story that was about the power of story to shape public perceptions. For him the medium and the message worked in concert. He understood that the process required more than stating facts. Yusufi needed to be credible, articulate, and compassionate. His story was as much about who he is, as representative of a community, as it was about the details of the unfolding case.

Yusufi's audience included persons directly touched by the bombing and violence, emergency workers who were called in to help, citizens and members of his faith whose communities were deeply affected, officials with a governing job to do, interested members of the public at large, and of course the press. The interplay of story, teller, and audience could not be predicted in advance, much less controlled.

As we write, the Boston Marathon bombing story is still alive in the news. We were curious about Yusufi and his role in recent events, so we called him again.

Yusufi told us he was sticking with his story.[46]

> *We are Bostonians first, and we speak from that perspective. We tell a narrative of what our institution, our community, is about: teaching and preaching an American Islam, an Islam that's rooted in compassion, that's rooted in commitment to our community and to America. We continue trying to tell that story in creative ways, explaining that we have a food pantry on Saturdays as a way to serve the whole community, and we have ESL courses.*

The question we most wanted to ask Yusufi was *how* did he perform as Storyteller-in Chief? Martha is very attuned to dealings with the press, and she knows the difficulties in giving narrative answers to yes-or-no questions. How was Yusufi able to tell the story he wanted to tell, in the way he wanted to tell it, and have an impact on public perceptions of Muslims in Boston?

> *When we were among the reporters it was very hard to go into narrative because they just wanted answers very quick, so I couldn't do it there. I think just the fact that I spoke English in a kind of fluid way surprised people and challenged their stereotypes.*
>
> *So we would spend time one-on-one with reporters and then invite them into the mosque. . . . and share who we are, and we would begin to see a shift in their attitudes and understanding.*

One reporter from the Boston Globe, Lisa Wangness, spent weeks and then months with us. She got to know us, our previous Imam and me, and now she doesn't report on the usual stuff. Now she reports on us like on any other Boston congregation. She just highlights the narratives on our leaders.

I think in a crisis it's hard for people to get to know you fully, but after the crisis subsides, I think you have the opportunity to tell your story.

The situation faced by the Muslim community in the United States is enormously complex, given real or imagined ties to Muslim communities all over the globe. Yusufi has fielded questions from all corners, from Jewish leaders curious about ties with the Muslim Brotherhood in Egypt to the FBI wanting to know about radicals. Here is how Yusufi answered questions about the Muslim Brotherhood in this way:

Here's the reality: A lot of the folks who initially came from Egypt were connected to the Muslim Brotherhood, because that's 25% of Egyptian society. They learned activism back home and they started doing activism here. But as they became more a part of American society gradually they realized that the way the Muslim Brotherhood operated was problematic, and those affiliations started to dissolve. But that doesn't mean that people don't have family, and it doesn't mean they are living out the perfect agenda here.

Even the Muslim Brotherhood has begun to change and has evolved as an organization. Some really amazing parts of the younger generation in the Brotherhood are that they eschew all kinds of violence.

We are a growing community. We're going to mess up at times. We need you to know that there is nothing evil going on here. In our group we sometimes do things that aren't very strategic and don't make sense. Help us figure that out.

When the FBI asked him about radicalization, Yusufi answered in this way:

We say there is no predictable pattern to radicalization; so designing a program around radicalization doesn't make sense.

Then we take it one step further and tell them we are countering all forms of unhealthy behavior by trying to project the right vision of Islam, rooted in compassion, mercy, and commitment to America.

Remember, a lot of our people come from repressive countries where there are no civil societies or civic institutions. Even the notion of funding your own mosque—the government pays for everything back there.

You guys need to realize that to the extent that we build strong institutions, we will be countering radicalization. You need to support us to do these things by not sending informants and by allowing community to happen.

Both the Boston police and the FBI have been very receptive to this, they get it. At least the people that we have relationships with are starting to get it.

We asked Yusufi about how he presented himself emotionally—how he let people in on the fact that he is committed to the United States, serious about what he believes, and irked by having to defend his community.

Usually I try to be very calm, genuine, and sincere. The passion for this work comes across because I truly am passionate about it. I love this work. I feel like we are in a historic place in the Muslim community where we are pioneering what a mosque space in America can and should look like.

But I will tell you that there is also a deep-seated anger that exists in me, because I hate that I have to answer questions about extremism and terrorism. It's not fair.

More recently I have begun to share that emotion with people, where I will say, "I appreciate what you are asking but a lot of this is just wasting time. The best thing that can happen is if we have strong institutions that communicate this message in robust ways. And you want me to use my time effectively towards that."

More recently I have started to experiment and let people know: It is deeply frustrating that you are coming to ME, asking me questions about terrorism. If you really want to know about extremism and terrorism, maybe you should ask a terrorist. I'm not one of them.

Yusufi did more than answer our questions about being a Storyteller-in-Chief—he gave the role a face. His narrative is exquisitely a story about stories and the way they can shape understanding—and sustain community.

Yusufi's storytelling was *intentional*, as it needed to be. Storytelling competes with many other forms of managerial communication. The organizational theorist Yiannis Gabriel explains that most outfits and entities routinely communicate without any narrative whatsoever. Press releases, broadcast announcements, regulatory postings, formal reports, numerical scorecards, rule books, and the like—all serve useful and even necessary purposes, but they're never sufficient modes of communication in a crisis. Storytelling is a lost art in modern culture. Gabriel concludes: "Organizations are not storytelling communities."[47]

We see this as an opportunity.

In a crisis, when leadership matters most, a story will be a deviation from the norm, a combination of reality and hope. The organization is likely to sit up and listen. When a leader acts in a new way because it is, in fact, a new day, organizational expectations are more likely to be hopeful than ominous.

In what follows, we offer three broad ideas. This section is not intended to be a list of storytelling competencies or a storytelling formula—beware of such things. Our aim is to remind you of skills you already have and concepts you know. Perhaps we can pique your curiosity about something you haven't thought of that will help you be a more effective leader.

Find Your Voice

Johnny Cash's daughter Roseanne always wanted to write Appalachian story songs. She felt blocked until she wrote "The House on the Lake," with images about her father's house in Tennessee and his death. She had discovered that "the more specific you are about places and characters, the more universal the song becomes."[48]

Leaders need not enroll in a course to learn about myth, language, or drama to qualify for Storyteller-in-Chief. Telling stories is inherent to human beings. When the psychologist Peggy Miller made live recordings of families living in Baltimore, she discovered that stories among preschoolers and their moms occurred *every seven minutes*! No doubt simple stories without sophisticated structures, but true-life stories told by mothers and children, nonetheless.[49]

The storytelling impulse doesn't cease at the front doors of our homes. Stories rain down on us. Think of what is being said in hallways and at the water cooler at your place of work. Think of the stories you've shared standing in line waiting to vote or see a movie. What about stories told as you watch the high school ballgame or parade? Everyone does it. Storytelling is how we connect the dots in our lives and the atoms in our brains.

A story takes an organization on a journey about people and their work, their learning, evolution, and growth. It includes specific names, faces, places, and things. In a crunch, unedited stories or anecdotes from the past won't work, and replacement stories won't suddenly appear on the spot, but they will emerge, and they will evolve when they're retold. This progression mimics the development of consciousness and unfolding of civilization.

We advise leaders to begin with a personal reflection. "I got the call in the middle of the night . . . I was shocked . . . I ran out the door . . . I had to think of something, and this is what I did." A story begun with the leader's experience can transform a cool directional message expressed in management terminology into a warm tale about human endeavor.

Start practicing. Now.

Pay attention to the reaction of the audience. Find settings and groups that welcome and appreciate personal stories, and deliver. Develop an ear to sense when the story-portions of your impromptu talks, factual reports, or formal presentations are having an effect. You don't need to be lyrical or theatrical. But you can always improve how you shape your stories to establish rapport and make your points. Share the truth of your experience positively and without pretense.

When you are fully present as an adult human being, you narrow social distances among all of us. Find your voice. Bring us together and help us heal.

Be *in* Your Story

Leadership depends on narrating an organization's new story while speaking about one's own. Who could truly tell the story of a massive external change without reflecting internal changes too?

Leaders have to own up to their vulnerability. The organization needs a going-forward story but won't hear it unless leaders have rawness in their voices. Two realities are present, a shaky now and a different future. You can't envision a better future and enlist others to go there with you unless you're in sync with what's happening today.

Steve Denne at Heifer comments that in the wake of crisis, "All eyes are on you. So, how you behave has multiplier impact—good or bad."[50]

An organization is always best served when it trusts its leaders. Self-disclosure builds trust. When leaders reveal their vulnerabilities as human beings who laugh and love and feel pain just like everyone else, we are more likely to trust them.

It is up to you to tell more about how you're responding—so everyone can feel free to respond in ways that are real for them too.

Sometimes leaders feel apologetic about being overly engaged. They feel embarrassed for getting carried away. They struggle if they feel they are not appearing confident in moments of despair. They mistake impassiveness for resilience. But if storytellers "omit the pain," suggests Marshall Ganz, a grassroots organizer now at Harvard Kennedy School, their "account will lack authenticity, raising questions about the rest of the story."[51]

Our counsel is to forego negative self-talk about feeling weak and exposed. Being vulnerable in the moment is the single most important element in finding your voice. Be *in* your narrative. Be the actor you tell about in your story as a living, breathing, feeling human being, and your listeners will join you where you want to go. The enduring principle of storytelling is, "Any emotion tends to be socially shared."[52]

Your authenticity is in the spotlight. Your actions are speaking louder than your words. As Howard Gardner explains, leadership stories need to be lived and not just told. "The individual who does not embody her messages will eventually be found out, even as the inarticulate individual who leads the exemplary life may eventually come to be appreciated."[53] You *are* leading by example. Be transparent, trustworthy, and real.

Tell your story in an engaging way that transports your organization toward restoration. Recognize the variety and volatility of emotions in the audience, and avoid gushing facts without the connective tissues of emotion and meaning.

And never tell a story with the intention of pointing the audience to a specific frame of mind. It's not for you to cheer people up, clear the air, or heal the wounds. Don't steer listeners toward your preferred conclusions, leaving little room for audience interpretation or disagreement. Heed this warning given by the management scholars Mary Jo Hatch, Monika Kostera, and Andrzej Koźmiński: "The danger in trying to control other people's meanings is that you become for them a symbol of manipulation and deceit."[54]

Be modest and never absolutely sure of yourself. In their influential examination of the challenges leaders face in managing unexpected events during complex times, Karl Weick and Kathleen Sutcliffe suggest you "remain in doubt that you're doing the right thing."[55] By staying ambivalent you'll increase the amount of information you take in. And you won't overpromise, issue ungrounded assurances, or default to simplistic black-and-white answers.

Years ago, Harry attended a consulting skills workshop with Peter Block, a mentor and guiding light, where the activity involved was to be videoed and critiqued to increase self-awareness. When Harry's turn came to be observed and commented on, Peter said, "Look at that!" Harry gulped.

Peter said, "Look at that ambivalence." Harry thought his nascent career as a consultant was about to take a turn in a new direction.

Then Peter brought it home. "And isn't it beautiful!" For Harry it was a new angle of apprehension: Ambivalence is an ally especially when there are multiple possible outcomes, audiences, media, and moments in which to act.

Finally, asserting that *your* meaning is *the authorized meaning* is an official act of hubris. Glimmers of coherence may come in flashes, appearing and disappearing, blinking on and off like the lights on the *Auriga*. Better to be unsure, open, and mindful. Stop, look, and listen! Let the facts unfold and be raggedy. Remember, if you make perfect sense in a chaotic situation, you're probably clueless.

At a community shelter where Harry volunteers, the sign on the wall says: "Be humble. You may be wrong." It is much better for a leader to be *in* the story as a humble human being, wondering *about* what's best for people than to *be* the story people are wondering about.

Just Tell It

If there's a singular moment for a leader to lead, it is under the pressure of a crisis. The simplest instruction we would give you is simple and straightforward. Just tell the story. Model and exhibit courage, engage others, and challenge everyone to respond and recover. You renew your authenticity when you stand up in a crucial moment and call the organization to its full potential.

No matter how difficult it may be for you to recount the details of a disaster, it's in everyone's best interest to reveal them openly. Suppression of painful events merely transforms a Rogue Wave into something *undiscussable*. You don't want your silence about the past to become a conspiracy that inhibits your organization's ability to move on and prolongs its psychological distress.[56]

Instead, go public with the story.

Story is like a flint and a spark that can start a backfire—the kind that burns fuel in the path of a wildfire and limits its reach. When a leader addresses a crisis with story, the narrative enters the organizational conversation. The Rogue Wave has been collectively experienced and now everyone owns it. Your stories at once belong to you and to everyone in the organization.

Storytelling is a recursive process. Meaning is made for all and for one simultaneously. Your story spirals out to others and returns, and then it repeats again. Anyone can retell it. It's now in everyone's hands, and everyone benefits. It's a crucial connection after calamity.

The force of the experience dissolved previous boundaries about who is in control of making sense of things. This is an opportunity to engage everyone in meaning making, an opportunity that is not to be missed. A Storyteller-in-Chief can create an enduring sense of community by turning collective experience into a narrative that reenacts and reinforces shared promises and desires. The story reconnects people and purposes.

So, be the Storyteller-in-Chief. Relish the position. It's the hot seat, the most important vantage point in the room, the chair of wisdom, and the home base for action. Grab the bullhorn, mike, or keyboard, and start telling the story! Trust in your ability as a storyteller. It is resident within you. You can do this.

Around the Campfire

When we, Harry and Martha, lead workshops on crisis leadership, we ask participants to tell stories while seated in a circle of chairs. The arrangement is a symbolic campfire with ancient significance as a place where elders, scouts, pilgrims, or travelers huddling against the cold gathered to sustain each other. In the circle, groups recommit to shared values and purposes and consider what to do next. The circle is not a hierarchy. The circle means we all belong right here. This is our space to be together as a community. Collective power derives from the stories we tell, retell, and hope are passed on. Our narratives give us solace and resolve. The circle reminds us we are facing life together. No wonder that in a disaster, storytelling is a community resource like no other.

6

Whitecaps on Canal Street: A True Story of Crisis Leadership

And God said, *Survive. And carry my perfume among the perishing.*[1]
—Tony Hoagland

Our perspective leans heavily on the value of stories and storytelling for leaders in the aftermath of a Rogue Wave. This has been confirmed in our interviews. Indeed, we have been startled by how many of our questions were answered with narrative. We have not yet spoken about a feature of stories that helps us use them to enrich our lives. It is the *coda*, a means by which the story is reinforced or embedded.

Jerome Bruner suggests that the coda "returns the hearer or reader from the there and then of the narrative to the here and now of the telling."[2] The coda acts as an invitation to the receiver to notice what's interesting in the situation and in the storyteller's particular use of words. The coda is not an explicit lesson but an invitation to insight. The coda can be a moral, a final word, or as we intend here, an encapsulating story. The burden rests with readers and listeners to discover for themselves what lies beneath.

The story we share in this chapter is neutral on what a leader *should do* in a Rogue Wave. We offer no list of actions to check off. No watch-outs or must-dos. How-to is up to you. Nor is the story a history lesson—it is his-story. Read it to be transported into your own experience and reality.

When we heard the story we were moved by the narrator's robust determination in the face of tragedy and despair, and we've been absorbed in its truth ever since. In its aftermath, we've questioned the depth of our own personal commitments to our communities, the potency of our leadership purposes, and the accuracy of our self-awareness. We have retold the story many times in audiences large and small, and haven't plumbed all its poetry. We know it by heart.

We tell this story by quoting or paraphrasing the narrator's words, interrupting occasionally to reinforce themes from earlier chapters. This leadership story is not unique among what we heard in our interviews, but it's one of the clearest examples.

But first, who is Rod West?

Rod West is an executive with Entergy Corporation who, in August 2005, was an operational leader charged with turning the lights back on in New Orleans after Hurricane Katrina. He's an athletic man in his forties who moved to New Orleans as a young child. He is African American, a husband and father, and he has a great resume. He was a football player on Notre Dame's 1988 championship team under the renowned coach Lou Holtz. Rod returned to the Crescent City after college to earn both a law degree and later an MBA from Tulane. He's active in many local associations and charities. Rod is now executive vice president and chief administrative officer at Entergy Corporation and on the board of directors of the National Football Foundation.

As a storyteller, Rod is candid and articulate even when recalling tough moments. He's reflective, composed, and searchingly honest. Rod's byline is, "Life is what happens to you when you are making other plans."[3]

We were privileged to have heard him tell it and now we're grateful we can retell it in written form.[4]

The Rogue Wave

For me, the moment of truth was not the actual storm in the Gulf of Mexico when we said, "Oh My God! A major storm is coming." It was the day when the levees broke and the 17th Street Canal gave way.

I got a call from our command center at the Hyatt Hotel. If you remember, there was a scene in "Jurassic Park" where the guy is looking out his rearview mirror and there's a Tyrannosaurus Rex. The mirror says, "The object in the mirror is closer than it may appear." Imagine that scenario, where one of our guys is doing damage assessment out on the street and calling us to tell us there are whitecaps coming down Canal Street.

I remember that visual because prior to that time, everything that we had done was done according to the book and how we drilled it. One major part of crisis management has to do with preparation. Until that time we were in control because we had prepared and drilled for scenarios up to and including catastrophic events.

The scales tipped after the 17th Street Canal flooded because that is the moment, the cascading event that led to the entire city—the landmass—being flooded. And so we did what we do according to the drill. We sent the crews out of harm's way.

I took the helicopter tour. It was just my boss, Dan Packer, and me. We were the two Entergy execs left on the ground, while the rest of Entergy leadership were in their assigned storm locations throughout the region—Jackson, Baton Rouge, what have you. I hadn't seen my wife and family in about four days. And they had not heard from me. So I'm taking a helicopter tour, and I remember looking down from 5,000 feet and thinking, man, the winds must have really been bad because all I see are the square foundations of the homes.

As I begin to descend to a lower altitude I realize I wasn't looking at what I thought were bare foundations. I was looking at rooftops! The background that gave me perspective for this visual was water, not the ground. The water was so high in these areas, I thought I was looking at foundations when I was looking at roofs.

That was the pivotal moment for me in terms of the gravity of the crisis. It went beyond the drill scenario of safety and security for my crews. That scene, that visual, and the emotional reaction to it . . .

My pilot had just come from tour in Iraq. We had the open microphone headsets, and he's literally sniffling. His name was Todd. I remember that: Todd and Rod. I remember him saying, "I've seen towns destroyed, and I've see chaos and mayhem. But this is the United States. It's always us doing it to somebody, or somebody else doing it to someone else, and we're coming in to help. This is the United States! Oh. My. God!"

By any measure, Hurricane Katrina was a rogue event. It was a series of unexpected storm surges that drowned 80 percent of New Orleans, making it impossible for everyone to escape to safety. More than 1,800 perished. On the day before Katrina made landfall, the National Weather Service warned that areas in the path would be "uninhabitable for weeks." We know now that they were very wrong. Vast sections of the Lower Ninth Ward are still uninhabited, unless you count stray dogs and snakes.

As costly as it was deadly, Katrina was a civil engineering catastrophe. Nearly every levee was breached. The experts had been fooled, and no one was really prepared. Lives and livelihoods were lost, and for the survivors there was extended chaos. Among American storms, Katrina was an archetypal Rogue Wave: sudden, spontaneous, and significant, and unrivaled in its destruction.[5]

Like everyone else, Rod didn't comprehend how Katrina would be different than previous hurricanes. Rod and his team at Entergy were as experienced, seasoned, and prepared for a storm as anyone. They had planned for emergencies including the flooding of New Orleans. They had drilled and simulated responses. They knew what to do. And along with everyone, they were swamped by reality. Katrina broke the gauge.

Name It

The tour was about an hour and a half in the air. I fly to Baton Rouge. I spend about 30 minutes with my family saying I'm okay, and then I go and meet the 400 crewmembers plus their families who were staying over in Baton Rouge at the Jimmy Swaggart facility, where they were holed up. Under normal circumstances, we stage our crews around the region in various places close enough so that they can come back to the city and begin restoration after evacuation after the storm passes.

They knew I was coming, and word spread.

Imagine the scene. They knew that I had been in the middle of chaos and mayhem. They had only seen pictures on CNN. But CNN only showed a block away from my command center, where everyone is on generated power, trying to survive. They didn't know. So imagine, I hit the front door and word is out: "Rod's here, Rod's here." And they start coming into the auditorium area from all over. If they were at the grocery store, they were dropping everything and coming to see me. I waited 30 minutes for everyone to get there.

Invariably, everyone wants to know, hey, how are things out there? What about uptown? What about my neighborhood? How bad is it?

In their minds, they're trained to go to the staging area for two to three days tops, the storm passes, and they come back to the affected areas, whether they live there or not, and they spend the next week or so restoring power. And they are heroes. Of course they'll never get the power on as quickly as the customers want us to, quick enough, fast enough—but of course they come back because this is what we do. This is our job. So they bring clothes for two to three days, as is the case. But of course this time is unique in that their families were there because it was a mandatory evacuation.

As I'm going through my assessment, I'm reacting in real time to the emotion of what I've seen. I lay out the level of devastation of what I saw from the air. Of course they knew that the Ninth Ward was hit pretty hard. They knew because of the (flooding of the) 17th Street Canal that parts of Lakeview were hit pretty hard, and none of that was surprising.

But then they started asking me about the different neighborhoods. My response was: "Six feet of water; eight feet of water . . . ."

"What about St. Bernard's—you know right where I live?"

"Nine. Feet. Of water."

Questions were being fired in rapid succession because the anxiety level was being raised as I'm letting them know just how bad it is. And finally I said, (slowly) "The city is under water. So for most of you, everything you left at home is destroyed."

That number was about seventy percent of the people in that room. Everything that they had left behind was gone.

Rod named it. Without sugarcoating or shirking, he told the straight truth in a direct manner. He could not be misunderstood. "Nine. Feet. Of water."

Imagine the situation. Entergy's first responders learn from their leader that their homes are gone, yet they must suit up, leave their families, and go to work on behalf of the city. They could not go to their own neighborhoods first. When the leader has named it, the truth is shocking. This wasn't rumor or television. Rod told them and he told them directly. He waited for all of them to hear it together. He himself was leaving a family, heading into the unknown of a command center in New Orleans and sleepless nights on the floor. Everyone was absorbing and coping with the impact of events in real time.

Face *Now*

As I'm looking at their faces coming to grips with reality, at that moment, I felt the oppressive weight of having to command the lives of the people who were in my charge while being responsible for their lives and livelihood. It was an epiphany about leadership—both the authority I had because I was their boss and the responsibility that I had for their lives.

I knew before I walked into the building that I had to tell them probably the worst news that they could hear outside of the health and welfare of one of their loved ones, and turn right back around and tell them how we've got to go to work, and rebuild neighborhoods that you don't live in and for people you don't know, when you're not sure how and whether you're going to have a roof over your own head or how you're going to feed your family.

I park it psychologically and candidly suppress the externalities of the storm: the dead bodies, the devastation, the darkness, the fear, the crime, the danger. I'm focusing on the leadership part. And that was the moment when it didn't matter what I was facing, that the only thing important was that I lead in both my words and my action.

I cried with them on that late morning. But I had to stop, and I had to stand up, get back behind the podium, gather myself, and say, "Alright, here's the plan."

I immediately had to focus and give them focus on what our job was. And I had to tell them, "We will find a way and figure out all the rest." Right now we can't control it: issues with insurance companies, issues with mortgage companies, issues with schools—all of that stuff was going to play itself out.

But I needed them to know first and foremost: "You and your family will have a roof over your head. We'll figure that out. But there will be no rebuild of New Orleans unless we find a way to do what it is that we do under these circumstances."

Rod stared directly into the gulf of pain that he and his people were experiencing. He joined them in their fear and grief, crying without regret or shame.

And then he faced their most pressing concerns, short-term survival and long-term purpose. He reassured his team that their most basic needs would be met, and he challenged them to rebuild New Orleans. Middle ground issues would have to wait. He didn't confuse things or make hollow promises.

Rod's leadership meant facing the brunt of the storm and its impact on people. He took responsibility. He chose to lead with empathy, truth, and decisiveness.

Face *Tomorrow*

We had employees going into the homes that their parents lived in to find their parents upstairs in the attic, dead. "I gotta get back to the house. I gotta get back to the house. I hope my mom and dad left. I hope my mom and dad left. Oh my God! They're in the attic."

We weren't just the first responders. We were the first ones out there. We were out there trying to figure out just how bad it was. We were the ones leading the police and the fire and the rescue folks. We knew the neighborhood, and we were here. So when I tell you that these employees rose to the occasion, there's a part in there that they didn't have a choice about.

But trust me when I tell you that not everyone made it.

I knew that I was in real time in the middle of an American saga. I knew historically the U.S. had not seen this level of singular devastation since the rebuild of Europe post–World War II in terms of the level of devastation, not caused by military but by natural disaster.

I felt like throughout the entire time I was in the middle of a movie being made. I knew that I was a player in the movie. But I had to discipline myself to not get so much into character that I lost perspective on what it was and where my work was relevant in the debate.

Every day I'm sitting around a conference room table with members of the military and members of city and state resources, and the whole issue of rebuild of New Orleans was as much political as it was physics. From a physics perspective, an electrical engineering perspective, we learned a fundamental principle at six years old when Mom told you that water and electricity don't mix. "You could shock yourself."

Well, we started from the fundamental premise that we would start working in the area that was dry. That happened to be the original settlement of New Orleans, the crescent. We called it the "Sliver on the River" and "The Crescent City." Let's start there since it's dry, and let's follow the water table north and east as the water subsides.

Now that made all the sense in the world, but the original settlement of New Orleans is predominantly white, and well-to-do. It's the older area of the town, aka old money, the blue bloods. That's an overly broad brush but that's the picture.

The areas of the city that were most devastated were predominantly black. So imagine the irony. Mind you, I'm having to go around to the different cities, to explain to the "refugees," citizens of the United States of America, why they can't come home. And they were, not unlike my own crews and employees at the time, accustomed to a two- or three-day evacuation (or maybe a week if it was really bad) and then they would come home. They were accusing me of conspiring with the white elite to keep black people from coming back to New Orleans.

When I talk about that narrative, there was a physical infrastructure rebuild, but there was also an emotional/political dynamic that played from New Orleans all the way to Washington, D.C.

Katrina was a full-scaled *American saga*. Rod's team was oriented regionally and devastated personally. Nevertheless, Rod grasped the larger picture, the broader dimensions of the Rogue Wave. It was a natural catastrophe with shattering human consequences, *and* it was an epic story for the nation. He was aware of the tragedy, the irony, and his team's role in history.

Rod and his team had work to do. First, on a scene that was their home turf, they performed triage. They pointed, directed, and steered emergency efforts of all kinds. They could not go home for rest—home was temporary housing. All the while they were exposed to heartbreaking discoveries.

Rod's game plan was rational in inception but political in its consequences. Rod knew they had to begin on dry ground and proceed into wet. It was basic physics. But who would have foreseen how Katrina layered racial injustice on top of an already stricken city? Rod was plunged into a human maze as bewildering as the flooded streets. Yet he had to carry the story to the wounded. He didn't flinch, and neither did he lose his compassion.

Rod coped with a reality that increasingly implicated him as an African American leader, an Entergy executive, and a loyal resident of the city. The contours of his role were larger than the power grid, but he didn't blink or turn away.

Dark Nights of the Soul

I was a member of Lou Holtz's first recruiting class at Notre Dame. What I fell back on was Coach Holtz and all of the lessons that I had learned in Little League and high school and in college playing football, basketball, baseball, running track: In the heat of the battle, when fatigue or fear or overwhelming circumstances would make cowards of most men, when you are ready to break, the only thing you can fall back on are your fundamentals. Focus on the WIN concept: What's Important Now. Right Now. Not any of this extraneous stuff, but what are the most important things to focus on, right now?

I remember I only got to sleep in two- to three-hour increments at various points of the day. We had an air mattress in the command center because the Hyatt didn't have power for a long time other than a two-megawatt generator.

To give you a sense of my purpose and the impact that it had, I literally left my wife and family on the Saturday before the storm, and sent them away. The storm hit in August, and they did not come back until the Monday before Christmas.

When they came back, I gave them the unabridged tour of New Orleans. I had access to the whole city. I showed them houses off their foundations, houses blocks away from where they were, and the Lower Ninth Ward that got so much attention.

We were coming back across the bridge, headed to the house, and they're in tears. And I'm looking at my ten-year-old through the rearview mirror—her name is Simone—and I say, "Simone, what do you think?"

And she wiped her eyes, looked up at me through the rearview mirror, and said, "Dad, we have a lot of work to do."

A ten-year-old, a ten-year-old! For her to have that perspective, which voiced my raison d'être at that moment, was so awe inspiring and invigorating—it affirmed all the hell that I had lived through. And honestly, I viewed it as a sign from God, because I needed that at that moment. The decision not to bring my family back was not an easy one, particularly when I had options to do a whole lot of other stuff elsewhere. That was one of those defining moments that I'll never forget.

Witnessing widespread devastation and distress was a long dark night for Rod. The WIN model drove out doubt and indecision but didn't salve his pain. For that he needed the support of a coach, his daughter, and the accumulated strengths from his upbringing and experience—his character.

Even leaders sleeping on the floor don't need to feel isolated. They take better care of themselves when they're open to help from all channels. Rod spoke at length about how he coped, what his reserves were, and how he felt about his role. He had been through other demanding situations in his life. It's a measure of how deeply shaken he was by the Katrina experience that he dug so deeply to extract lessons.

All throughout my life I've wondered why things happened the way they did. I always felt as if there must be some sort of calling because I've lived a charmed life, notwithstanding my socioeconomics or other circumstances. When Katrina hit, there was a calm, I felt WOW, all the things I've gone through have prepared me for this. I would not have wanted anybody else in the position other than me. That's how focused and prepared I felt.

I was always struck by Robert Greenleaf's notion of servant leadership. That resonates with me to my core. Besides this whole notion of leadership capability, Robert Greenleaf's notion of servant leadership actually gave some structure to my sense of purpose.

I discovered Greenleaf probably five years or so before Katrina, when I was leaving the practice of law and coming into the corporate arena. My father had died in 1998. He was electrocuted planting a tree in the backyard. My father's death literally was a wake-up call for me to examine my life. I was about to turn 30. My career was on a path to being a very good lawyer in a law firm, and I always wanted to be consequential. I wanted the work that I did to be meaningful. Being a lawyer was what I did, not who I was. A lot of things changed in terms of focus. His death was a life-changing event for me in that my perspective on what success means was not going to be how many hours I billed and how much money I made. I decided then that I wanted my life to be far more consequential.

It was during that period of introspection after my father's death when I was introduced to Robert Greenleaf.

It was like, "I get it."

This is the life I've lived and it has shaped my perspective so much that I'm not easily moved or rattled because I have seen so much. And there is perspective. His death changed my perspective on everything. Not just leadership, but everything . . .

I'm sure my narrative plays out in the lives of so many people. Candidly I got joy from taking my board of directors, or Chamber of Commerce members, or business executives, or Wall Street investors on an unabridged tour of the city, where I'm giving them real-world narrative. They would marvel at how far

New Orleans had to go—they'd see the waterlines on the buildings. I would have to stop them—they're all in tears and shock and amazement—and I'd say, "You have no idea how far we have come." That's the perspective I still have for this city.

There are a lot of people who've laid claim for having done this or that. I am one of probably a handful of people who could tell you who were the pretenders and who were the contenders when the real chips were down.

Make no mistake; I'm a work in progress like we all are. Every change I have is an opportunity to deepen, widen, and expand my point of view on things.

Rod was ready for what might show up. He was keen on taking what he could from a situation and pushing its limits. He would not say he exploited the crisis of Katrina, but clearly he did not waste the storm. Hard times developed the muscle of character and the wisdom of experience. With that attitude, the dark night of the soul is experienced as a prelude more than pain.

Pre-Resilience

The reasons why I think it's an advantage to have played competitive sports are (1) the significance of training and preparation and (2) it separates the pretenders from the contenders in crisis leadership. You don't know that you have a well to draw from unless you've been forced to go to that well to discover it. That well is a psychological well.

The only way I could describe it to you is that it's in your training, in your intuitive practices. You're running wind sprints for conditioning with your teammates. Or you're going through navy seal training or boot camp or something where you are being pushed physically and mentally to what you consider to be the brink of your capacity to endure. Whether it's a matter of pride or desire to not let your team down, or just your dogged determination not to fail, you push yourself to the brink.

You hear terms like "gut it out," or "suck it up," or you found that well that you drew from got you through that adversity. You come out of that experience with a different psychological swagger. You discovered something about yourself that you didn't know was there because you were forced to endure.

It's this ethos that people in the military, people who have played sports, people who fought wars, people who've been through similar catastrophic events together have. There's a look that you give each other, a nod of acknowledgment. For those who have not gone through it, no other explanation would really suffice, and for those who have gone through it, no explanation is necessary.

That's what I fell back on. Adversity reveals character—it doesn't build it. I saw the stress and the strain of Katrina manifest from the front line police officer to the White House. I saw personally or heard on conference calls the stress and strain of that catastrophe in the day-to-day exchanges of men and women in positions of authority and responsibility . . .

In some respects, I had to grow up early. My mom and dad divorced when I was in first grade, and we moved to New Orleans. I had a younger sister.

I remember my mom reading to me a missive from Jenny Langham, my teacher, back when report cards weren't A, B, C letters, and the missive was flattering stuff, but she talked about how it was striking to her that at this young age I possessed a leadership presence about me that belied my age.

I had to go look up "belied my age." I didn't know what that meant. My mom said that Miss Langham says you act much older than you are. And I looked at her with the "huh?" I was truly a second-grader, mind you. I wasn't some sage or savant, but the implication for me was that I was looked at and expected to be different. I was looked at to be strikingly upright as a leader.

I was always that guy—student council president, 4-H club president. I wanted to be first in everything, not because I wanted to beat some guy or gal in front of me, but I felt like that was where I was supposed to be.

So I guess my point is: somewhere along the line you demonstrate a capacity to lead early on. The old adage is: if the dog is going to be a biter, you will know it when he is a puppy. So there are certain characteristics that I had to assume are apparent early on or are revealed through adversity.

Rod had a deep well of pre-resilience. Shaken by Katrina, he maintained a deep and inner confidence. He honored his upbringing and his experiences for the strength and personal will they gave him. He had absorbed positive messages from parents, teachers, and coaches. He wasn't relying on technical experts—Rod didn't mention lawyers, public relations professionals, or officials in his circle of support. His community was composed of people who had invested in him. In the darkest days of Katrina, he reaffirmed who he is and found a way through.

Even in the confusion and chaos wrought by Katrina, Rod stayed clear and connected to his core. He exhibited emotional self-awareness as he spoke of his coping mechanisms, his reserves, and how he felt about his role.

His example is powerful. When others believe in us, we believe in ourselves. When the chips are down, leaders who reach into their bank of community support are claiming what is already and powerfully theirs.

Helpful Help

The humbling aspect of Katrina concerns the men and women who were gas mechanics and line mechanics and supervisors and tree trimmers. These were people who were working every day in neighborhoods. Some neighborhoods were where they lived, but for the most part they were working elsewhere and weren't sure if their neighborhoods were going to get rebuilt. They were living in temporary housing.

Candidly, the thread that kept everybody together and kept us all from breaking down was the single-minded sense that if we were not successful in doing what we were doing, the city didn't have a chance. This transcended the hierarchy of the company.

The lineman and the vice president were on equal footing in that we had all suffered rather equally. Katrina didn't make distinctions in her wrath. Who your family was or where you went to school didn't matter. So there was a single-minded purpose of rebuilding the entire city for the greater good.

The single-minded focus was certainly necessary and it was also a distraction from the pain and loss. It was cathartic. It was very much a crutch upon which we leaned. You worked sixteen hours that day and when you were off you had eight hours to sleep. But, really, you had five hours to think about what in the hell am I going to do? What is going to become of me and my family and my neighborhood?

Entergy made sure nobody missed a paycheck. That was profound—just like gravity in terms of keeping people whole and doing business continuity. Collective psyche . . .

I remember Coach Holtz calling me in the midst of the chaos, because apparently word had gotten back to him that I was on the ground—maybe I had done an interview at CNN or something—and he offered to send a plane to come and get me. I said, "Coach, no, I got this. It's about trust, love and commitment, right now."

"Trust, love, commitment" was the motto of the 1988 championship team. We went undefeated, and on our ring—I'm wearing it right now—on the side, it says, "trust, love, and commitment."

"I trust you. Do you care about me? Are you committed to excellence?" That was what we asked each other and anybody in our personal or professional lives whom we would rely upon or who would rely upon us. If you could answer yes to those three questions, then you had a winner on your hands.

Rod's coach offered to come to his rescue. Rod downplayed this part of the story, but it reflected a deep and natural temptation in a lousy time to look for another line of work. It's instinctive to be self-protective by choosing another fight, another day. Rod was quick to say he was staying put and why. He remained at his post because he was there to lead as a member of his community. That's who he was. He had panic under control. *I got this, coach.*

Rod responded in the manner of a trained and competent professional, but as he told his story, he dwelled less on how he gave directions or managed resources and logistics, more about managing the logistics of the soul—love, trust, and commitment. He was focused on his organization and community, on people, and on relationships.

Helpful Help is a constant thread in the story. Rod recognized the efficacy of collective effort. He knew that by working together on a shared cause he was granting others gifts of agency and purpose. He also recognized the intangible value of tangible actions such as getting paychecks to people. In a shattered world, a meal is more than nutrition.

Storyteller-in-Chief

Of all the physical feats and managerial moves Rod pursued, none was more important than his storytelling. He led with empathy, by example and command, and he *restored* himself and his community through story.

Rod's role was multidimensional. On one hand, he had responsibilities and stature because of his professional role with Entergy. He had to think in terms of business, operations, and science. On the other hand, he was an African American citizen of New Orleans who understood the political and cultural dilemmas of his hometown, state, and nation. And of course, there were hundreds of associates under his wing, doing their jobs. Customers, citizens, and coworkers were on his leadership map, as well as stakeholders in the corporation and community. Rod never ducked or shirked the complexities. Rod told at least three interwoven stories to three audiences, simultaneously.

The Victims' Story

The victors and the survivors tell our story. We honor the life of the folks who didn't make it by making sure we tell the story, we tell the truth.

There was nothing romanticized about the devastation. When we were talking to the communities, talking to town hall meetings and in Washington D.C., we had to make sure that the reality of what was going on in this town and this region was understood, viscerally. Let's be clear, the victims in New Orleans in particular who were hardest hit economically, tended to be people of color. In the rest of the country the initial reaction to the victims of Katrina was not, "Omigod, it sucks to be them." It was, "They live below sea level. Why in the hell do they live below sea level?"

The initial story made great for ratings for CNN, but after a while people moved on to other things. We had to make sure that the country understood that this wasn't a tornado that hit a few blocks and a few families were affected. This debilitated an entire city. That required telling the truth from the start.

"Telling the truth from the start," is one of the great lines in the literature of leadership. Look what it accomplished here. The truth ("nine feet of water") enabled the Entergy team to engage in its fearsome duties. The truth ("if we were not successful in what we were doing, the city didn't have a chance") respected the victims and honored the casualties. The truth ("water and electricity don't mix") cut through the complexity of decisions and choices. The storyline of truth telling created a foundation for recovery, recuperation, and renewal.

Rod's motivation for telling the truth was critical. He straddled many worlds, understanding and respecting them all.

The devastated poor weren't simply victims of a terrible weather event. They were already suffering from poverty and racism. That did not mean they should be patronized or victimized further. Citizens, employees, responders, shareholders, and politicians had no claim to optimistic guarantees. Everyone *did* have a right to hear the truth about what had happened and what might happen in the future. False expectations needed to be crushed for the common good.

Rod articulated from the beginning what was really at stake, the rebuilding of New Orleans. And in the cacophony after Katrina, he was heard.

The New Orleans Story

You were not going to rebuild the city the way it was. You had to have some predictive analysis to determine the likelihood of a certain area of the city being repopulated because that was going to determine whether you had a realistic chance of getting a return on the investment, versus building in an area that was going to continue to be vacant.

When you think about the factors of repopulation, there are things you take for granted when you choose a neighborhood: grocery stores, and schools, electricity and water.

These folks on the outside looking into the city viewed the reason that they couldn't come home was only because they didn't have power. (On the other hand) the business standpoint was that it wouldn't be prudent for either the government or for us as a utility to make an investment in an area that was not likely to come back. We knew empirically the factors of return were not there.

But the customers didn't know it. They believed we were the catalyst for the comeback. There was this unhealthy tension between the obligation to make prudent investments and also to make a product that the customer viewed as part of their life.

The narrative I told was that the only thing I would do for you, by providing lights to the neighborhood that you lived in, was to illuminate just how bad it is in your neighborhood. I am not the reason you can't come home—but I do know you don't have a chance if I'm not successful in making power available.

I called this an "unhealthy tension" because of the psyche of the most important stakeholder—the communities we served. They were debilitated. But I also knew they were not going to be able to come home in the time horizon they desperately wanted because the infrastructure they left was gone, and it would be a long time before normalcy. They had to survive in the interim, but the company had to survive as well.

Making power available is not the same as having power being used. Making power available was not the solution. It was a catalyst to any repopulation efforts, but it was not the singular issue.

Expectations had to be reduced in every way. The path of the rebuild had to follow the water line, going from where the water was shallow to the point where the water had been deep, and there was an increasing scale of devastation moving from shallow to deeper water.

Now that narrative is one of physics, and from a rational standpoint it makes sense. But politically and geographically I was moving from well-to-do neighborhoods and white neighborhoods to black neighborhoods north and east. You can imagine that dynamic playing out in the context of a rebuild where everybody wants their neighborhood to come back first, or at a minimum, you have your crews working every neighborhood at the same time.

I was having the conversation about what was possible with the engineers. You had what was possible being layered with what was prudent. The probabilistic analysis of repopulation was the physical condition of this area of town and its houses, schools, businesses—is the problem just a function of electricity? Or will we have to come here and rebuild communities? And then, how long will it take?

We were essentially doing damage assessment, not only of our electric and gas infrastructure but the entire city, because it was informing our point of view for the case to rebuild. From my vantage point, it was a painful reality. The people we served on August 28th were devastated on the 29th, and at least two-thirds of them had no idea how bad it was.

Because we never left, we went through it. I had eyes in the sky because of the helicopter, and along with the mayor, the federal government and the military was able to see it immediately. We were all processing the information and, even in the darkest hours, planning how to respond.

Communications to the outside world was an evolution. As the shock and immediacy of Katrina began to give way, we wondered what to do from here? Is New Orleans going to die? Or is it going to live? And if so, will it be different? How will it come back? What are we willing to invest in it? Will the people come back?

Rod carried a story that was unfolding, aging, and picking up new complexities. The story evolved and enabled listeners to grow in their understanding and acceptance of what was at stake for New Orleans.

Rod knew that a complex crisis in a community could not be reduced to a simple storyline. If he had strayed from the facts, he would have limited his influence and jeopardized what he was trying to do. He refused to soften the story of Katrina's impact or pretend that it was only a natural disaster. The story of Katrina was more than a snagged thread—it concerned the ripped fabric of a city, region, and country.

The Entergy Story

Entergy's corporate headquarters had relocated to the Jackson, Mississippi, area. The real issue for us was whether or not Entergy was going to come back to New Orleans as our headquarters.

This was a conversation not just with our employees, but also with the board of directors. The issue was not whether we wanted to come back, but whether we could or should come back. It was tied to our point about whether New Orleans was going to come back. Entergy as an organization had its business continuity plan already in place, because the move to Jackson was all about business continuity.

The question was always, what will the new normal look like?

We have Entergy Mississippi, which is a good corporate presence in Mississippi. Mississippi was rightfully interested in having us stay there in perpetuity. At the end of the day, the board and the company's leadership made the decision that we wanted to come back home. Entergy, the corporation, is larger than New Orleans. The corporation would be fine either way, but since New Orleans is our home, Entergy's role in New Orleans was going to be critical to the rebuilding of New Orleans.

I think the employees of this company collectively believed that they would be critical to the resurgence of the city of New Orleans. The board took the educated leap of faith not only that New Orleans would return but also that Entergy's presence was critical to that return.

Those were the kind of moral and ethical conversations we had as a team. I credit that to Wayne Leonard, our CEO, our board of directors, and the leadership team of our company.

I was boots on the ground. I recall very vividly making a presentation to the board of directors on New Orleans from a clinical perspective. Imagine my talking to our board in clinical terms—not impassioned—on the factors of population. I used the theme of a gumbo, making a gumbo. New Orleans was viewed as the Gumbo Coalition. The gumbo's ingredients were used as the theme for the rebuilding of New Orleans. First you make the roux or the base, that being the infrastructure, where I talked clinically about the amount of levies, the gas and electrical infrastructure, the telephonic infrastructure, the housing stock, the buildings. As you added each ingredient to the gumbo, I talked about another aspect. Each one of those ingredients was a component of the rebuild.

I ended with the video from the director of FEMA, who told the New Orleans first responders and emergency operations personnel that it was going to take three to five years for New Orleans to return to a sense of normalcy, but that the infrastructure was a critical component. I remember that vividly, because that's what I closed with. At no point did I want our bias in the presentation. The board had to decide about relocation of the corporate headquarters.

Leading remarkable performance in challenging times requires dedication to core values. Entergy's board and executive suite wrestled with values questions as they struggled to make the best decisions for the enterprise. Moral and ethical issues were woven through the scientific and business questions. Rod found ways to tell the truth in a clinical tone, and also with the vivid and visceral imagery of a gumbo—archetypal for New Orleans. It all worked. Through story, Rod led leaders.

The Aftermath

In terms of what happened since Katrina, we can approach it through a set of lenses. One lens would be me, one lens would be the organization, and one lens would be the city.

For me, having gone through that crucible, I came out on the other side. Having gone from a clinical, sort of academic experience of overcoming adversity in athletics that was notional, I came out of that Katrina experience with the conviction of the importance of leadership, the importance of preparation, the importance of team, and the importance of fortitude, the importance of vision.

I progressed because of the success of things we accomplished that I either led or was a part of. We rebuilt the electric grid. We rebuilt the gas grid. We were one of the cornerstones for the rebuilding of the city's critical infrastructure, and we got Entergy New Orleans out of bankruptcy because of the work we did on the regulatory front. The commercial objective of business continuity was real. I played a leadership role. My career benefited, and I was asked to rebuild the company that is Entergy New Orleans. In 2006, I became CEO, and my job was to continue the build-out of the company in conjunction with the rebuild of the city. After 2009, I was elevated again from president of the operating company in New Orleans to the Office of the Chief Executive, as executive vice president and chief administrative officer, for Entergy Corporation.

The successes of the response to Hurricane Sandy were 100 percent a result of the lessons learned from Katrina. I can tell you personally, in everyone's playbook in the northeast, there's an Entergy wing of the playbook library. We complied lessons learned. We were the blueprint. It's been an affirmation both professionally and personally that consequential leadership matters . . . .

As for the city, New Orleans no longer talks about itself in a post-Katrina mindset or ethos. We now define ourselves by our aspirations as a city. We commemorate Katrina, as we did on the ninth anniversary on August 29th, because we recognize that was a critical point in our city's history. For Entergy and the City of New Orleans and this region of the country, we've moved on and are moving on.

Our goals define us now.

You can have leadership qualities, but there is no substitute in terms of going from confidence to conviction in terms of the significance of leadership. More importantly, I learned the most from witnessing the lack thereof.

I'm comfortable in my conviction that leadership matters.

Rod emerged from Katrina with a boatload of wisdom. His career has progressed. There's been recognition and reward for his inherent and hard-won leadership strengths. His narrative can be illuminating for aspiring leaders as well as leaders in crises.

Entergy New Orleans survived bankruptcy and has a brand as a public, for-profit player with worthy social goals. Entergy Corporation is at the forefront of utilities that consider climate change, safety, and assistance for low-income customers, and it has stayed put in New Orleans. Rod is proud "to work for a company with a conscience."[6]

And what about New Orleans? Judith Rodin reports that New Orleans 10 years later has a much better flood defense system, fast-growing repopulation, a new school system realizing dramatic improvement in student performance, and according to a school board leader, "a renewed spirit."[7]

Rod's story is a coda for leaders and their Rogue Waves. It's complex and provocative, it points at progress amid pathos, and it lacks a tidy ending. For us, it's an invitation to our readers. Draw what you will from Rod's narrative and, better still, tell yours.

The Calm *after* the Storm: Trauma, Growth, and Renewal

Rough waters make a good sailor.

—seafaring proverb

Returning to the "original" Rogue Wave story, the *Auriga* arrived at Dutch Harbor, Alaska, on Friday morning for round-the-clock repairs.[1] Angie told us:

> *I don't think you give yourself time to sit down and process. We were out the next Sunday afternoon. One moment to the next, there are 10 things that you are busy doing, but you just keep going. Like now, we sit around and have a beer and laugh about all the insulation that was floating around. But then, we didn't really process it, any of it.*

Kale explained:

> *We were with a very dynamic group of individuals. Everybody on the boat has done very well. They were all a good bunch of guys to have a crisis with. We do go through that pass quite regularly. I'm very much aware of what could happen. You look at the geography. On the north side of the chasm it's about 30,000 feet deep and on the south side it's about 30,000 feet deep—it's nearly vertical. Very steep. There's a tremendous amount of water movement anyway, but I think the thing that hit us had to be traveling at a super, super rate of speed. Honestly, today I don't think there is anything I would have done differently.*

Angie added:

If all things were equal, we might decide to choose a different pass. But, we wouldn't avoid the pass. But, if it's no big deal we might take a different route.

Shortly after the wave incident, one of the sailors decided to get out of the industry and sail yachts. Kale continued:

I used to say in the early days of crabbing that when the pile of stories was bigger than the money, it was time to get out. We financially had to stay in. It's been tough at times.

Kale admitted he was most concerned about his wife, Angie:

I knew she was scared—I think everybody probably was. I kind of made a little promise to her when I went down the stairs to get all the guys and go to work. I said, "We are not going to get in that water, don't worry we are not going to get in that water" and abandon ship. At that point, I don't know why I was confident, although we did have plenty of survival suits in that particular situation. I would say that safety wise we are (now) very cognizant of what can happen. If there's a choice of having one survival suit or paying the extra money for two, we are over the top safety-wise. We have lots and lots of safety gear.

Angie reflected on what, if anything, they gained from their near-disaster:

I think there might be examples, a couple people on the crew, who might say, "I don't want to do that again." But, I think there were attitudes that "We just made it through that. If we can make it through that, we can make it through anything."

That was the most horrible thing I can imagine. So in the next crisis that happens on the boat, we are going to be levelheaded, clear-headed—we'll think our way through it and deal with whatever happens. So I think there's a psychological strengthening that happens.

"The Bering Sea is a helluva place to hang out," Kale admits, but he is still a Bering Sea captain. To put things in perspective, Kale concluded his tale with an anecdote about the dangers of being back on land:

After being a Bering Sea fisherman forever and ever and ever, we saved up five or ten thousand dollars, and we went in to an investment company, and we were sitting across from this guy. First of all I didn't meet the requirement for the minimum amount of money, so I was kind of shot down, but he proceeded to tell me how dangerous being in the stock market was, and he kept using that term "dangerous."

I remember looking at the guy as I was leaving, and I said, "There is nothing apparently dangerous about this at all. There is nothing dangerous about this. I don't even have a pair of boots on. I'm sitting here in my street shoes. This is not dangerous."

Captain Garcia has told his story "about ten million times," and no doubt others have retold it. The Aleutian rogue wave/Garcia Rogue Wave tale focuses our attention on what matters most and it is leadership in a crisis. Kale's awareness of what was happening in the moment, his concern for wife and crew, his ability to make good decisions under extreme pressure, and his self-confidence strike central themes of our book.

There *is* a calm after the storm. Spending time "to sit down and process," in Angie's words, often yields the realization that "psychological strengthening" has occurred. But that is not always the case. Here's a different story, a case where leadership showed up not at all.

On May 12, 2015, Amtrak Train 188 mysteriously sped up to more than twice the posted speed limit on a steep curve in Philadelphia, and derailed. The train was carrying 243 people—at least eight died, and more than 200 were injured. Josh Gotbaum, an expert in emergency management, was a passenger on the train. When the train rolled over, Josh "realized we could die."[2] He suffered broken ribs and lost his glasses but was able to climb over dislodged seats and jumbled luggage and escape through a window that was now on the ceiling.

Gotbaum is genuinely knowledgeable about disasters—he was the founding CEO of the September 11th Fund, the Chapter 11 trustee who rescued Hawaiian Airlines from bankruptcy, and the former CEO of the federal agency charged with saving pensions when companies become insolvent, among other roles. Reporting as both victim and expert, Gotbaum gave high praise to the first responders, the Philadelphia Police Department, and the medical teams in the emergency rooms. As for Amtrak, "in my view, our national train company failed almost every single test."[3] Gotbaum's focus is not on what caused the crash, but what happened afterward—who was ready and who stepped in.

Gotbaum is critical of Amtrak in three ways that implicate leadership. First, the railroad was demonstrably unprepared to handle the crisis. There were no procedures in place for what to do to reach out to victims, eventually settle claims, or even answer basic questions. Second, employees were untrained and unable to go beyond their narrow job descriptions when talking with victims and thus had to pass them on to the next department to get additional information. Third, Amtrak's CEO never showed up at the hospitals or the derailment location. Gotbaum concludes that an overhaul is needed at Amtrak, not by cutting the budget while leaving board and management where they are, "but to do the reverse."[4]

The Red Cross and the City of Philadelphia were right there for the victims, up close and personal. But there was no human face to Amtrak in the aftermath of its Rogue Wave.

It doesn't have to be this way.

From Rogue Wave to Renewal

For years we, the authors, have been busy coaching leaders. In some of our leadership development workshops, we use a simple exercise. We ask people to draw a line that shows the progression of their development as a leader. In every case this leadership lifeline is a curvy slope. Their stories usually begin with a starting point of school or a first job. Their lines tend to tilt upward from there, but never in a straight incline. There are hills and valleys. The hills represent successes of one kind or another. The valleys are the setbacks.

We encourage reflection with questions such as these:

- When have you been shocked or surprised?
- What did you learn from the hills? From the valleys?
- Were you able to foresee the next shift upward or downward?
- Who or what was most helpful to you as you traveled this journey?
- What conclusions can you draw about your leadership?

One of the most suggestive questions we ask is, "What were the key events for you as you traveled from one high point down through a trough and then up to a place higher than where you started?" That was essentially the meta-question in our Rogue Wave interviews.

We've heard story after story about an ordinary day interrupted with a sudden swoop downward into the chaos of an organizational crisis. Then the story turns to a slog back up, finally reaching a place where hard-earned benefit (for both leader and enterprise) was credited to the experience. People want to extract some redemptive quality from the experience, and we sensed they often shared their stories with that intention. Leaders, no matter how deep they dig, have a difficult time concluding their narrative with failure or diminishment.

A pattern in their stories is evident. The down part of the cycle was guaranteed. The rise back took pluck and luck. When we map this journey, we replicate the shape of a change curve. Attributed to Elisabeth Kübler-Ross to depict the stages of death and dying, the change curve has proven to have explanatory value for individuals and groups experiencing change. We rediscovered this timeless shape and took an additional step to overlay the six major pieces of the Rogue Wave puzzle. Our chapters follow a sequence that matches the change curve, beginning with the Rogue Wave itself.

Chapter 2, *Respond*, captures our injunction to name it and face it. Dark nights as described in Chapter 3 require a leader to *Reflect*. Helpful Help, in Chapter 4, means to *Reach* (for help as both giver and receiver). The subject of storytelling in Chapter 5 emphasizes the need to *Restore*. Then there is *Renew*, the Holy Grail, about which we will have more to say presently. The complete cycle of Rogue Wave to Renewal is depicted in Figure 7.1.

For leaders, the explanatory value of this depiction comes in several flavors. Most important, there is a *sequence* that cannot be ignored. When this order is violated in several known ways, the leader/organization is in failure mode. For example, moving too quickly into the future when the battle is still raging may be dangerously dreamy avoidance of the Rogue Wave and its impact. If you are not taking time to reflect on how your team as well as you have been battered and bruised, and to reach for help, you don't really know what's going on.

When you skip Reflect and Reach on your way to Restore, you risk being dismissed as shallow and superficial, and you limit your organization's ability to heal. Of all the mistakes we heard about or witnessed in the dozens of organizations where we have worked, this mistake is the saddest. A leader who shows fear of organizational and personal pain makes things worse.

An oft-used word we heard was compartmentalization. Walling off feelings of fright in order to function does work—in the short term. Eventually, making feelings verboten in an organizational conversation imposes a heavy cost. People check out. They resign, or they disengage. Lights on, nobody home.

Similarly, there is no route to Renew without passing through Restore. Without meaning and purpose, organizational improvement is iffy. Assuming the role of Storyteller-in-Chief is job number one for leaders in the aftermath of a Rogue Wave. Remember how Rod West (in Chapter 6) embraced this role for the benefit of his associates and stakeholders.

Stories are usually told in linear fashion, but then reality isn't story. Life has loops and swoops, repetitions and returns. Reflection after a Rogue

Mapping the Journey:
From Organizational Crisis to Leadership Maturity

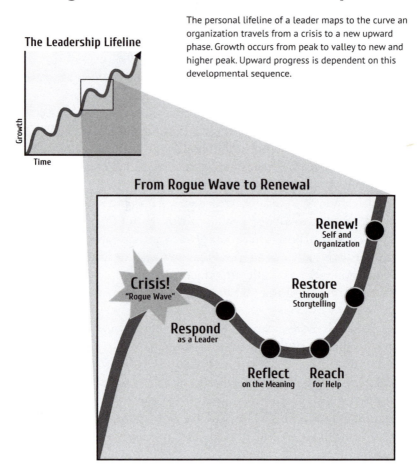

The personal lifeline of a leader maps to the curve an organization travels from a crisis to a new upward phase. Growth occurs from peak to valley to new and higher peak. Upward progress is dependent on this developmental sequence.

The Leadership Lifeline

Growth

Time

From Rogue Wave to Renewal

Renew!
Self and
Organization

Crisis!
"Rogue Wave"

Restore
through
Storytelling

Respond
as a Leader

Reflect
on the Meaning

Reach
for Help

Figure 7.1

Wave, and reaching for help, iterates. As much as Harry's mother, Betty, advises whiners to "build a bridge and get over it," one never gets over psychological injury. Best case is to include a Rogue Wave experience in our understanding of who we are. Perhaps the best way to read the points on the map is to see them as bases that must be rounded. Skip a base, even when you think you've hit the ball over the fence, and you'll be called out.

Another way to use the model is to help in the *delineation* of phases. For example, Respond is top priority in an emergency. The leader must name it and face it right this moment. Responding is discrete work.

If it is intermingled with Reflecting, it's lost. A leader can't call time out and take a walk in the woods to get it together when the forest is on fire. Rod ran from his helicopter tour to his gathered group. There was no time to waste.

Similarly, to Restore through storytelling requires conscious effort and prolonged practice to get right. Coming to grips with personal anecdotes and macro themes in a narrative and speaking it publically is of a different order than being at someone's bedside and listening compassionately. Even so, be mindful of the spiral nature of Rogue Wave work. Listening to the organization also yields stories the organization most wants to hear.

There is an unacknowledged theme to the model we've created. Like it or not, hills and valleys are emotionally loaded. The direction up on the curve evokes feelings of hope, increasing confidence, comfort, and even excitement. The direction down is a fall into negative emotional space where we experience frustration, confusion, misery, shame, and perhaps dread. This relative repulsiveness or attractiveness of the journey's direction is a measure of *valence*. Negative valence creates negative expectations and avoidance. Positive valence does the reverse.

The importance to leaders of understanding this psychological phenomenon is twofold. First, people vary in how much or little they are attuned to valence. Being emotionally up or down may be a function of the situation, or the personality, or most likely in the mix.[5] Leaders would do well *not* to infer the worthiness or resilience of an associate based on reaction to a Rogue Wave. Compassion and certainly discernment about people are called for in a cataclysm. But to infer that a weepy person is therefore weak, or a stolid person is therefore strong, is an unnecessary error. Rod cried with his team. Would he have been more leader-like by showing a stiff upper lip?

The other insight that valence provides is that storytelling can induce positive momentum. Positive expectations create attraction. When a leader speaks believably about better days ahead and makes a promise not to waste the crisis, ambivalent followers will get off the fence. A story with purpose at its center will gain adherence and organizational traction. Rod West's positive purpose determined the positive outcomes. Saying "it's up to us to rebuild New Orleans" inspired hundreds of workers to perform over and above any reasonable expectations.

The flip side is that not telling a story at all, or spinning an implausible narrative, increases the likelihood of unwanted outcomes for all.

Finally, the model exhibits a path forward, a *direction* toward a preferred outcome. Our intent has never been to prescribe delineated steps toward post–Rogue Wave Growth. Nor have we intended to make optimistic claims about what leaders may accomplish when the chips are down. The stories we heard are as complex, as immense, as nuanced as human experience. We would do them injustice were we to distill them into the six things you must do to succeed. Our coda matches Rod West's "telling the truth from the start."

Nevertheless there's an inferred course in what we heard in our interviews. Upward. Toward the light. The destination is renewal. The goal is wholeness.

Wholeness is a big word that includes learning and loss, openness to the human condition, inclusion of people and contradictions, alertness and awareness. We can grow from the truth of our experience at every point on the curve.

But before we consider how to make additional strides upward, we need to pause long enough to scrutinize the aftermath of Rogue Waves. We know that Kale Garcia emerged hale, healthy, and sanguine from his experience. We know that Vincent Scully remade his school for the better. We heard Rod West tell us that there can be new life when waters recede. Patrice Nelson leads a healthier community shelter. Yusufi Vali is reshaping perceptions of Muslims in Boston. We heard many stories about personal growth and organizational transformation, and we want to believe that renewal is the base case.

We want our tragedies to transform us. There *must* be an upside to horror. We hope and pray that what doesn't kill us will make us stronger. Yet we know that every leader is on a unique journey. Every Rogue Wave has a specific impact. Each organization is like no other. No person reacts in the same way, and there is no single predictor or resilience. To discern a path from Rogue Wave to Renewal we need to discuss the difficult matter of *trauma*. Our intent is to brief crisis leaders on a subject that they can't solve yet can't avoid and would benefit from having foreknowledge about—human response to disaster.

The Utter Reality of Trauma

A classic experiment from 1949 has lasting implications for crisis leadership.[6] Jerome Bruner and his Harvard colleague Leo Postman explored *incongruity*—when what we expect to see happens to be shockingly, incomprehensively, different. The experiment toyed with the minds of Harvard and Radcliffe students, using playing cards. Not Tarot cards or hidden-up-the-sleeve cards, but regular old playing cards with some trick cards in the deck: a black three of hearts, a red two of spades, a black ace of diamonds, and so forth. When the time to recognize cards was measured, it was unsurprising that it took students longer to recognize the trick cards than the others.

There are several interesting findings, but for us two are most pertinent. First, sixteen of twenty-eight students were "disrupted" by the trick cards—perhaps even distressed? The subject who was most thrown into disarray said,

> *I can't make the suit out, whatever it is. It didn't even look like a card that time. I don't know what color it is now or whether it's a spade or heart. I'm not even sure now what a spade looks like! My God!*[7]

What can we make of this? If trick cards can cause a "gross failure" of perception and then panic, what might we expect of people—employees—in a situation where survival is at stake? We know that reactions to threats are unpredictable. The strongest people may not be most resilient, given the circumstances. We've been through all nature of organizational crises and been surprised every time by who keeps their balance and who melts. There's no correlation between one's value to the company and trauma. And also, as we continue to say, it's the size of one's psychic boat, not the height of the wave, that matters the most. It makes no sense to try and buck up suffering colleagues by diminishing the source of their misery. Try saying, "It's not that big a deal," to someone in tears.

A second finding from the card experiment points toward the persistence of our assumptions, the cussedness with which we stay in our mental swim lanes. Or as Bruner and Postman observed, we too easily "fixate" on what we expect to see because that's what we expect to see—nothing more—and then we see just that. One student called the black three of hearts a three of spades forty-four times in succession, another called it red sixteen times, and six students were never able to name the card correctly. Don't confuse me with the facts! Bruner and Postman recount the hayseed's reaction to seeing a giraffe: "Thar ain't no such animal."[8] No wonder it takes a Rogue Wave to disrupt deep organizational assumptions and unexamined thought patterns. Trauma—not to say we want to order it up, ever—may indeed be our friend, if it helps us get out of our own way. Michael Conforti taught us that trauma is not pathology; it's the "unfolding of destiny."[9]

Clearly there are differences between card tricks and death threats, yet when faced with incongruity small or large, our brains react in similar ways to close the gaps between expectation and reality. They are trying to restore order and calm us down.

In any case, it takes new meaning to restore meaning. Small violations can be easily resolved. After innocent pranks, surprise parties, and comedic tricks, it's: "Ha! We fooled you!" And we say, "Okay, I got it. No harm, no foul."

At the other extreme, when life or death is on the line, efforts to restore meaning are so profound, and variable, they resist psychological understanding. Our source for a definition is the American Psychological Association (APA)—not one of the 19,000 books about trauma for sale on Amazon: trauma is "an emotional response to a terrible event."[10] As for traumas related to disaster, the APA explains:

> *Disasters such as hurricanes, earthquakes, transportation accidents or wildfires are typically unexpected, sudden and overwhelming. For many people, there are no outwardly visible signs of physical injury, but there can be nonetheless an emotional toll. It is common for people who have experienced disaster to have strong emotional reactions . . . . Following disaster, people frequently feel stunned, disoriented or unable to integrate distressing information. Once these initial reactions subside, people can experience a variety of thoughts and behaviors. Common responses can be: Intense or unpredictable feelings . . . Changes to thoughts and behavior patterns . . . Sensitivity to environmental factors . . . Strained interpersonal relationships . . . [and] Stress-related physical symptoms.*[11]

Trauma wasn't always defined in this way, however. The word means "wound" in Greek, and although descriptions of trauma have been recorded as early as the Epic of Gilgamesh five centuries ago, it wasn't until the nineteenth century that psychologists began to examine a condition that is so perplexing today. Stephen Joseph, a director of the Center for Trauma, Resilience, and Growth at the University of Nottingham, describes the remarkable evolution in our understanding of trauma from what was considered a spinal injury among victims of train accidents—Charles Dickens was a casualty in 1865—to "soldier's heart" in the Civil War, "shell shock" in World War I, "battle fatigue" in World War II, and after Vietnam, the direct result of a terrible event. The APA has continued to evolve its view, and in its latest *Diagnostic and Statistical Manual of Mental Disorders*, trauma is understood as being related *both* to a bad event and to how the event affects us.[12]

This is a shift with significance. If trauma is less about the event and more about the response, less about conditions causing victimhood and more about the recovery of the victim—in other words, less about the wave and more about the boat—it is more open to treatment than otherwise. With trauma, treatment entails learning ways to exert some degree of control over how we feel, and that goes for organizations as well as individuals. If trauma encompasses both *what happened* to us and how we *experienced* whatever it was, its cause could be an office entanglement or a Katrina-sized storm.

Further, the traumatized individual could as easily have been an observer—watching television on September 11—as a participant on the street.

When leaders fully accept the responsibility to be in charge of the conditions under which people have entrusted their lives and livelihood at work, collective recovery from organizational trauma is their responsibility too. Just as ship captains are ultimately accountable for the safety and well-being of their passengers and crew, responsible leaders watch over their flocks. The buck must stop somewhere, and leaders' obligations *as leaders* places the physical and psychological welfare of others first, even at their personal risk. Yet expectations for what leaders can do to palliate pain must be circumscribed by realism.

Michael Conforti explains that there is an "utter reality" to trauma extending way beyond shock and awe. The reality is that it ruptures our illusions and shatters the world we want to see—and it never goes away. Full recovery from trauma is, in his estimation, a "secular miracle." Conforti's insights into trauma are transformative—they describe a realty that few leaders, or professional helpers for that matter, can see. Healing is making whole and accepting trauma as part of life. If we're not in Kansas anymore, we need to get on with living wherever the storm has dropped us.[13]

According to Conforti, the greatest thing you can say to someone after a Rogue Wave is, "I know you're suffering." Silence, then, is a virtue. When told more, a leader should listen more deeply, and perhaps add, "I know."[14] Leaders *can* do this.

Is there a continuum between small surprises and large, between shock and electrocution, between "thanks, I needed that" and full-blown posttraumatic distress? The worst case, posttraumatic stress disorder (PTSD), is defined by the American Psychological Association as "an anxiety problem that develops in some people after extremely traumatic events, such as combat, crime, an accident or natural disaster . . . where people relive the event via intrusive memories, flashbacks and nightmares; avoid anything that reminds them of the trauma; and have anxious feelings they didn't have before that are so intense their lives are disrupted."[15]

PTSD can be dangerous and deadly. The Afghanistan and Iraq wars have created a half million psychically wounded American veterans, and last year 8,000 soldiers and veterans committed suicide.[16]

The U.S. military is fighting back with resilience training. The army's Comprehensive Soldier and Family Fitness (CSFF) effort, begun in 2009 to combat increasing instances of suicide and mental illness, has spent $125 million to teach a million soldiers.[17] CSFF training has been extended to leaders as well. Stephen Brooks, the deputy to the garrison commander at Fort Belvoir where the army's first executive course was delivered, said, "This class teaches that resilience training has most dividends for younger folks, but it has a lot of value for everyone."

My initial impression was that it was related to suicide prevention, but I learned that it's really much bigger than that, so the benefits spread 360 around our entire mission. To me, the key to resilience is to be positive, and to look at life as a glass half full. As a result, people are a lot less anxious and focused on how to be better instead of spending energy wasted wringing our hands about what might happen.[18]

The war after the war continues, but the army has yet to determine which of its hundreds of resilience programs do the most good.[19] Meanwhile, harm is outspreading to care workers and trauma professionals in the form of compassion fatigue—burnout and emotional exhaustion. Accordingly, Naval Academy experts recommend that leaders vigorously practice self-care and self-compassion while ensuring that military clinical psychologists do the same.[20] In our language, there are dark nights to be faced, and everyone loses when leaders are oblivious of their needs, try to tough it out, or go numb.

Two of the most common ways to deal with trauma are cognitive behavior therapy—a way to talk yourself out of your painful feelings—and exposure therapy—a form of desensitization, where you are repeatedly confronted with your worst nightmare.

If trauma is an injury experienced in the body and not the thinking brain, however, there may be other, better treatments. Bessel van der Kolk, a psychiatrist who is head of the Trauma Center in Boston, is attacking PTSD from a new angle—to help people "find a sense of safety in their bodies." His methods are aimed at helping victims pass their traumas into memories so the memories can become mental "ancestors" and cease haunting the present. Van der Kolk uses physical techniques based on yoga and eye movement in his therapy, and results have been promising.[21]

What is pertinent for leaders is how PTSD has become the central paradigm of disaster reaction. According to George Bonanno, a professor at Teacher's College, Columbia, and his team, PTSD has "nearly engulfed all other considerations about the consequences and implications of disaster," including resilience, and healthy human response such as the expression of grief.[22]

The psychotherapist Patrick O'Malley, writing in the *New York Times* about his therapeutic approach to grief, posits an idea that leaders would do well to keep in store during organizational change. In his view, there is no one way to experience mourning a loss. "The truth is that grief is as unique as a fingerprint." The stages of sorrow are not formulaic, and the end of pain is not some sort of closure. Instead, by holding onto the memory of loss, we honor what was good, what we once loved, and what is now taken away.[23]

Here is the leadership point: Advising an individual or even an entire organization that it's time to move on after a disruption may disregard the natural process of recovery and healing. Impatience is not a virtue in those moments. An urgent timetable of expectation doesn't provide Helpful Help.

And to reemphasize, it's a costly error in judgment to see a person's reaction to loss or change as an indication of fortitude, or talent, or value to the enterprise. Sometimes the most stable people in a crisis are rattled. Perhaps they're feeling great compassion or sorrow and they are truly aware of what's really happening. Jack Welch, the former CEO of General Electric, is known to have said, "If you're not confused, you don't know what's going on." If you're not hurting, you're not in touch with what is happening.

Perhaps trauma *is* the human experience.

It may be that we process important life events outside of conscious awareness, which greatly complicates research.[24] Attempts to measure the unimaginable are bound to fall short. Sometimes there *is* no silver lining to a terrible event and the human response, the moral response, is to be present with suffering.

This is what a leader needs to know: Most people experience one or more traumatic experiences in their lives, but only five to ten percent develop PTSD. The best treatments for PTSD have not been proven, and the psychological community worldwide is furiously looking for better techniques. Resilience can be taught and learned yet the complexity of trauma continues to impede prophylaxis. There is no single pattern of disaster response—PTSD is just one of many that is possible. Others include depression and health-related symptoms, as well as ordinary human heartache and grief.[25] Finally, as Bonanno explains, trauma is not all of a piece. "Human beings are capable of great joy when they're suffering."[26]

Rogue Wave outcomes are beyond a leader's ability to predict. The calm after the storm is never assured. Yet for most people most of the time, growth emerges from the struggle to survive.[27]

Posttraumatic Growth

In thirteenth-century Persia, Rumi observed: "The wound is the place where the Light enters you." No matter the potential benefit with regard to enlightenment, no one is apt to pray for a wound.[28] Jerry Jacobs, director of the Disaster Mental Health Institute at the University of South Dakota, wryly observes that even if trauma were proven to be a platform for personal growth, "I wouldn't recommend it as a way of improving yourself."[29]

The aftermath of trauma is paradoxical, a mixture of the good, the bad, the ugly, and sometimes even the beautiful. These coexist, and most people most of the time experience at least something positive from trauma.[30]

Lawrence Calhoun and Richard Tedeschi, two of the original researchers in the burgeoning field of posttraumatic growth (PTG), have identified five domains of PTG and developed an instrument to measure their existence: personal strength, relating to others, new possibilities in life, appreciation of life, and spirituality.[31] Developers of these scales do not intend for their standardized inventories to capture the full range of human growth after trauma. PTG research, still in its infancy, has understandable trouble explaining the paradoxical nature of the phenomenon. In one study, for example, participants who reported that they had grown from a trauma experienced the world both as under their control and as a crapshoot.[32] One possible conclusion is that human development is more like a dance than a march—two steps forward, one step back—where the rhythm is ontological. The experience of finding meaning and purpose presents measurement challenges for the experts but may well be at the core of experience.

It is important to say that PTG is not just a matter of being resilient beforehand, coping successfully with events as they unfold, and thinking positively afterward—though these well-researched and frankly commonsense frames of reference are most certainly related to recovery. But we don't know enough about the complexities of human existence to arrive at anything approaching formula or nostrum.

We do know how meaning is central to sanity, to happiness—and to civilization. Meaning is present when we have expectations that interconnect people, events, objects, and beliefs.[33] When trauma disrupts what we think, feel, know, and believe, it is a new ballgame, or to the point, the game is over. It's as if the rules have inexplicably changed in the middle of a play but the score is still being kept—and we are losing. The way forward for all of us when we're suffering from shattered expectations and blown-apart assumptions is to agree on new and better rules to live by.

We do this where we can, by rewriting our stories. Isak Dinesen, the Danish storyteller and author of *Out of Africa*, has been often quoted saying, "All sorrows can be borne if you put them in a story or tell a story about them." In that vein, Bryan Doerries, "a self-described 'evangelist' for classical literature and its relevance to our lives today," stages readings of ancient Greek plays for veterans in order to complement conventional therapies for PTSD.[34] Doerries reminds us that Sophocles was both a dramatist and a general, and his audiences were soldiers. For a community in crisis, tragedy is "like an external hard-drive. You plug it into an audience and they know what to do." From articulated suffering, people find shared meaning in powerful ways. For Doerries,

> *Tragedy fills us with a sense of urgency that if we don't act immediately we're going to be bystanders to our own destruction. The stakes are that high, and that's the only way to break through the neurological, almost impenetrable armor of habitualized bad decisions. William James said that "in most of us, by the age of thirty, the character has set like plaster, and will never soften again." So it requires a shock to break through the hardened neurology of the pathways of our decisions over time. It requires a shock of discomfort that affects us physically and emotionally and spiritually.*[35]

Doerries's understanding of the narrative engine driving PTG is reminiscent of Victor Frankl's suggestion: "What is to give light must endure burning."[36] PTG offers relief from outmoded ways of thinking, the parts of our minds that have always resisted growing up, and from hard lessons we mis-learned. We can feel free, free at last from invisible chains binding us to our juvenile, injured, less-capable selves.

According to Jennifer Pals and Dan McAdams, "The life story should not be viewed as just one piece of the complex puzzle of posttraumatic growth, (as the PTG model suggests), but rather as the fundamental frame that holds the entire puzzle together."[37] McAdams, who is the author of the life story model of identity, admits that he too is still working on his life story. Now *this* is PTG-enhancing activity that lies squarely within the purview and purpose of leaders. "Narrative identity adds a new meaning to life," writes McAdams. "Through the life story the author is able to explain, for the self and for others, how he or she came to be and where life may be going in the future, integrating the reconstructed past, experienced present, and imagined future into a personal narrative that gives new meaning and purpose to life."[38]

Leaders in a crisis moment may have no *one* person to turn to, but they do have a leadership story. What they say to themselves about who they are and what they're all about in an hour of darkness makes all the difference. In our interviews with leaders, we heard again and again about parents, teachers, and early exemplars of wisdom who had backed them in key moments. Positive memories were integral to their identities. It was as if reinforcements were radioed in: I'm taking fire and this is my position.

To go from trauma to growth, Pals and McAdams describe the process as having two steps. First, acknowledge the "disequilibrating" impact of what has happened. No sugarcoating. No shrugging it off. No distancing. Instead, this awful/appalling/atrocious thing has happened, and there is no getting around it. Second, construct an ending that can be positive. Rather than saying we're all going to die, try this: We'll find a way out. We're in this together. Fear is our greatest enemy. As your captain, I'm with you.

When England was being bombed in the dark days of July 1941, Winston Churchill encouraged his countrymen and taunted the Nazis with this extraordinary line: "You do your worst and we will do our best."

Rogue Wave Renewal

Renewal after Rogue Waves combines two interwoven aspects of growth and development: leader-the-person renewal and organizational renewal. And in the cases of Yusufi Vali and Rod West, there is a third level of regeneration for their respective cities, Boston and New Orleans.

Max DePree, former CEO of Herman Miller, auteur of enlightened leadership, and author of *Leadership Is an Art*, keeps focus on what matters most:

> The goal of renewal is to be a corporate entity that gives us space to reach our potential as individuals and, through that, as a corporation. It cannot come about through a process of mere self-perpetuation. Renewal is an outward orientation of service, rather than an inward orientation of maintenance. Renewal is the concern of everyone, but is *the special province of the tribal storyteller* [emphasis ours].[39]

The educational leaders Bill Breisch and Marty Lexmond recently investigated the influence of growth after trauma on leadership.[40] They asked focus groups and individual leaders about how their growth was manifested after traumatic events, and they coded the responses within a theoretical framework based on the literature of leadership as well as psychological instruments that measure PTG. Their work delivered a model that fits our findings: leaders who grow after being traumatized by a Rogue Wave are likely to benefit in three ways—by becoming more purposive, more relational, and more adaptive and oriented toward learning. Throughout our interviews we heard leaders tell us about some of the distinctive ways they felt they had grown. Each has a precision and particularity to the person.

For example, Harry Schlough, an executive with experience in technology, early-stage investment, marketing, and other fields, clearly remembers a call in the middle of the night.[41] A turnaround effort for a failing company where he was one of the leaders had suddenly collapsed, threatening his sense of fiduciary responsibility to many stakeholders. It caused both an institutional and a personal crisis. "How do I maintain my moral and ethical norms with what this might mean? I looked in the mirror and asked if I could continue to lead, or should I? I need to really believe in it." Harry became more *purposive* about maintaining his moral framework. "I have a much greater understanding after that crisis and two or three others, having my eyes opened that morality is crucial . . . and it won't make you the most popular person in the room."

In another example, Charlotte Walker, a startup entrepreneur, former financial services CEO, and now COO at Doolli, told us about the "extreme embarrassment" she felt when a new technology on which her company's future rested was called out as a "terrible idea"—her response was to bring in her closest advisors, and seek a *relational* solution.[42]

Zoltan Csimma is a native Hungarian who was chief human resources officer at Genzyme when there was a contamination problem in a manufacturing facility.[43] Cell lines used for manufacture of some key drugs for rare diseases were contaminated. "The *Boston Globe* said we were putting junk into our product . . . We had a huge amount of trust with our patients globally, and it was eroded." It was difficult for all. Zoltan would "wake up at 2:30 in the night," his boss had bags under his eyes, and "you had to use every piece of leadership to keep your team motivated." Zoltan reflected how, after this event and many other difficult times over the course of a career in human resources, "I'm way more open minded now about people shifting careers and doing new things." He has become more *learning oriented and adaptive*.

In individual ways, each leader had grown. Each had learned something when the chips were down, when something unexpected or negative happened, when there was failure, or when they were just plain wrong.

The experts are not ready to nail anything down. After a thorough review of research Breisch and Lexmond concede that "[T]here is currently no literature that examines the area of how the growth as a result of trauma impacts various aspects of an individual's life in terms of specific outcomes."[44] Some of the stories we heard indicated positive change in both leader and organization. Recall the New England Center for Children, Urban Ministries of Durham, The B&O Museum, police departments, and organizational functions.

Jefferson Singer opens a window on how both the leader and the organization can experience transformation. A therapist and professor of psychology at Connecticut College, he describes the process of making stories to make meaning from experience, and then retelling them to extract more meaning. The sequence goes from story, to meaning, and then on to wisdom, providing a "surer and more graceful footing on life's path."[45] When a leader initiates the process of story/meaning/wisdom, both leader and organization can be on the path forward. The leader tells the story in the organization, it is retold by others, the leader amplifies and repeats, and on it goes in a virtuous spiral.

The research on this question of how communities make meaning following collective traumas is limited, but there is some. When the psychologists Roxane Silver and John Updegraff and their team interviewed 85 residents of a firestorm that destroyed 600 homes in Southern California in 1993, they found that over 75 percent of their respondents could find some meaning in the disaster. Over the following two years, people were asked whether they had searched for and found meaning, and if so, how. Half engaged in an active search for meaning, and more than 85 percent said they were able to make some sense of it—and it didn't matter whether they were direct victims of the fires and had lost their homes or not. "Those who had found meaning by 2 weeks after the firestorm reported significantly less distress over the next several years," and were less stressed over the following six months. Although the roles of local officials or influential community members were not studied, the authors asserted that the opportunity for leadership to accelerate meaning making and reduce distress was evident.[46]

After the attacks on 9/11, posttraumatic stress symptoms were reported by nearly half of Americans.[47] In order to grasp the nation's collective trauma, Updegraff, Silver, and E. Alison Holman performed a national, longitudinal study, following people for two years after September 2001. Americans were asked whether they were searching for meaning—over two-thirds reported they were, but only forty percent were able to find any.

People who looked to others for purely emotional support, or who went into denial, or who put a positive spin on events suffered more than people who sought and received advice that was relevant to their situations. The role of leadership was not considered, but again the question is whether a positive leadership presence, focused on tackling horrific realities, would increase meaning and reduce suffering. "The more people were able to find meaning, the fewer posttraumatic stress symptoms they experienced over time."[48] Most important, "[F]inding meaning may have served to restore some order or coherence that was—at its core—unanticipated, threatening to national security, and devastating."[49]

As empirical support for the value of leadership continues to grow, we do not need to wait for confirmation when we already know some strategies that work. We, the authors, elect a path to understanding organizational renewal that welcomes new evidence and values lessons learned from experience. And in any case, with Rogue Wave renewal, just as with our life stories, it's the context, stupid. "Culture calls the shots," according to Pals and McAdams.[50] A Rogue Wave is a crisis shared. How a leader responds, what narrative the leader constructs, and the nature of the better day collectively envisioned for the future, are deeply tied to the values, history, and ways of doing things that constitute a culture. In the immediate aftermath of a shock to the system, our leader is our proxy, the author of our shared reality. The unspoken cultural test is this: "Is our leader still one of us?" If so, only then are we willing to be led toward renewal.

Lead On!

Tom Yeomans said, "Anyone who takes on responsibility is on a hero's journey and is open to transformation."[51] Yet renewal has risk. There are no safe harbors in leadership life. You (and your organization) could be crushed by events, and regress. At least be mindful that Rogue Waves are always out there somewhere, and use alertness to your advantage. But does it really have to be like this? Do you have to experience pain to get a payoff?

The journalist Kathryn Schulz has pointed out in her meditation on error, *Being Wrong*, that rightness is satisfying but "it is ultimately wrongness, not rightness, that can teach us who we are."[52] Indeed, you can learn much from trouble if you choose.

Ron Heifetz, Alexander Grashow, and Marty Linsky, from the Kennedy School at Harvard, make solid recommendations for leadership survival in a crisis, echoing our work in describing dark nights during disasters. "Defining your life through a single endeavor, no matter how important your work is to you and to others, makes you vulnerable when the environment shifts."[53] The risks inherent in *overidentifying* with your role as a leader at the cost of becoming less human are at the heart of our message.

In the "Introduction" we noted that we were suspicious of too much irrational exuberance in discussions about crisis and leadership. Our cultural narrative is to celebrate heroes and exalt those who stare down adversity. We expect our leaders to take us forward, raise our spirits, and inspire us to do great things, no matter the odds. Yet in an environment of permanent crisis, leaders are encountering events they never imagined.

Our intent in this book has been to be *both* alarming and reassuring. As we see it, leaders can hold both terror and transformation as possibilities, and in so doing they generate redemption stories that may lead their organizations to recovery and renewal. The novelist John Barth once commented, "[A]s someone says in some story of mine, 'Our lives are not stories,' and, 'The story of your life is not your life; it's your story.' "[54] An interpretation is that it is good and healthy to separate who you are from who you think you are—you can change the latter if not the former. Another view is that your story *is* your life—as you develop your narrative, you will change who you are. When you lose sight of land, you can navigate by using either your life or your story as your compass.

We close with an excerpt from a well-known meditation, the so-called prayer of Sir Francis Drake:

> *Disturb us, Lord, to dare more boldly,*
> *To venture on wider seas*
> *Where storms will show your mastery;*
> *Where losing sight of land,*
> *We shall find the stars.*

What matters most is that once disturbed, you lead boldly on wider seas.

Notes

Introduction

1. *Time*, February 27, 1978.

Chapter 1

1. Norman R. Augustine, "Managing the Crisis You Tried to Prevent," *Harvard Business Review*, November 1995.

2. Steven Fink, *Crisis Management: Planning for the Inevitable* (New York: AMACOM, 1986), 21.

3. K. Bradley Penuel, Matt Statler, and Ryan Hagen, eds., *Encyclopedia of Crisis Management,* vols. 1–2 (Thousand Oaks, CA: Sage, 2013).

4. Erika Hayes James and Lynn Perry Wooten, *Leading under Pressure: From Surviving to Thriving before, during, and after a Crisis* (New York: Routledge, Taylor and Francis Group, 2010).

5. Ellen Gamerman, "How a Wave Swept the Art World," *Wall Street Journal*, March 20, 2015.

6. Charles Vincent, e-mail message to author, November 20, 2013.

7. Kale Garcia and family, telephone interview with author, December 22, 2013.

8. Gladden Schrock, e-mail correspondence with author, November 21, 2013.

9. Laurence Barton, *Crisis Leadership Now: A Real-World Guide to Preparing for Threats, Disaster, Sabotage, and Scandal* (New York: McGraw Hill), 11–14.

10. Ibid., 322.

11. Oklahoma City National Memorial and Museum Web site. http://www.oklahomacitynationalmemorial.org/index.php.

12. Larry Nichols, former CEO of Devon Energy, interview with author, March 14, 2014.

13. Barbara Perry and Harry Hutson, "Time Line," in Anthony Patrick Carnevale and S. Kanu Kogod, eds., *Tools and Activities for a Diverse Work Force* (New York: McGraw-Hill, 1995), 149–150.

14. Barry A. Cipra, "A Healthy Heart Is a Fractal Heart," SIAM News, 36, no. 7 (September 2003).

15. Ary L. Goldberger, C. K. Peng, H. Eugene Stanley, Plamen Ch. Ivanov, Luis A. N. Amaral, and Jeffrey M. Hausdorff, "Fractal Dynamics in Physiology: Alterations with Disease and Aging," *Proceedings of the National Academy of Sciences*, ISSN 0027-8424, 99 (February 2002): 2466–2472.

Chapter 2

1. Blasphemous curse uttered by surprised and angry sailors.

2. Robert Frost, "A Servant to Servants," *North of Boston* (New York: Henry Holt, 1915), http://www.bartleby.com/118/9.html.

3. Karl E. Weick and Kathleen M. Sutcliffe, *Managing the Unexpected: Assuring High Performance in an Age of Complexity* (San Francisco: Jossey-Bass, 2001), 78–82.

4. Mike Berardino, "Mike Tyson Explains One of His Most Famous Quotes," *Sun Sentinel* (Fort Lauderdale, FL), November 9, 2012.

5. John Kim, business executive, interview with author, December 20, 2013.

6. Ian I. Mitroff, *Why Some Companies Emerge Stronger and Better from a Crisis: 7 Essential Lessons for Surviving Disaster* (New York: American Management Association, 2005), 42.

7. Ibid., 43.

8. Norman R. Augustine, "Managing the Crisis You Tried to Prevent," *Harvard Business Review*, November 1995.

9. Eric J. McNulty, "What the Ebola Crisis Can Teach Business Leaders," November 25, 2014, *strategy+business* (blog), http://www.strategy-business.com/sb-blogs-strategy_and_leadership.

10. Gerald Lewis, *Organizational Crisis Management: The Human Factor* (Boca Raton, FL: Auerbach Publications, 2006), xi.

11. Jeffrey Kleinberg, "Building Individual Resilience and Organizational Hardiness: Addressing Post-Trauma Worker's Block," in Earl Hopper, ed., *Trauma and Organizations* (London: Karnac Books, 2012), 256.

12. Ibid., 260.

13. Ibid.

14. Javier P. Oyarzún, Diana Lopez-Barroso, Lluis Fuentemilla, David Cucurell, Carmen Pedraza, Antoni Rodriguez-Fornells, and Ruth de Diego-Balaguer, "Updating Fearful Memories with Extinction Training during

Reconsolidation: A Human Study Using Auditory Aversive Stimuli," *PLoS ONE*, 7, no. 6 (June 29, 2012), doi:10.1371/journal.pone.0038849.

15. Daniela Schiller, Marie-H. Monfils, Candace M. Rao, David C. Johnson, Joseph E. LeDoux, and Elizabeth A. Phelps, "Preventing the Return of Fear in Humans Using Reconsolidation Update Mechanisms," *Nature*, 463 (January 7, 2010), doi:10.1038/nature 08637.

16. Jack Zenger and Joseph Folkman, "You Have to Be Fast to Be Seen as a Great Leader," *Harvard Business Review* (blog), February 26, 2015, hbr.org.

17. Erving Goffman, *The Presentation of Self in Everyday Life* (Garden City, NY: Anchor Books, 1959), 249.

18. Noam Shpancer, "Overcoming Fear: The Only Way out Is Through: To Get Rid of Fear, You Must First Embrace It," *Insight Therapy* (blog), *Psychology Today*, September 20, 2010, https://www.psychologytoday.com/blog/insight-therapy/201009/overcoming-fear-the-only-way-out-is-through.

19. Tom Dreesen, comedian, quoting Frank Sinatra, *Late Night with David Letterman*, March 30, 2009.

20. Lani Peterson, professional storyteller, interview with author, February 25, 2014.

21. Travis Proulx and Michael Inzlicht, "The Five 'A's of Meaning Maintenance: Finding Meaning in the Theories of Sense-Making," *Psychological Inquiry: An International Journal for the Advancement of Psychological Theory*, 23, no. 4 (2012): 317–335.

22. Steve Brigham, former president of America Speaks, interview with author, January 21, 2014.

23. Wilfred R. Bion, *Experiences in Groups and Other Papers* (New York: Basic Books, 1961), 91.

24. Ibid., 84.

25. Jeanne C. Harasemovitch, "Conversations with Shades of the Past: Turning Ghosts into Ancestors," paper presented at Scientific Meeting, San Francisco Center for Psychoanalysis (September 9, 2013), http://sf-cp.org/sites/default/files/scientific_meetings/2013-2014/ConversationswithShadesofthePast.pdf.

26. Nathan Koppel, "Fraternity Chapter Closed over Video of Racist Chant," *Wall Street Journal*, March 10, 2015, A5.

27. David Boren, Twitter post, March 9, 2015, http://twitter.com/President_Boren.

28. Augustine, "Managing the Crisis."

29. Morela Hernandez, Chris P. Long, and Sim B. Sitkin, "Cultivating Follower Trust: Are All Leader Behaviors Equally Influential?" *Organization Studies*, 35, no. 12 (2014): 1867–1892.

30. Chester I. Barnard, *The Functions of the Executive* (Cambridge, MA: Harvard University Press, 1938).

31. Vincent Strully, CEO and founder of the New England Center for Children, interview with author, April 14, 2014.

32. Anthony Mason, "Back from the Brink," *CBS News Sunday Morning*, January 31, 2010, 10:06 am EST.

33. Tony Vaughn, business executive, interview with author, December 11, 2013.

34. Stephanie Streeter, former CEO of Banta Corporation, interview with author, February 14, 2013.

35. Frank Lloyd, associate dean, SMU Cox School of Business, interview with author, November 26, 2013.

36. Robert C. Townsend, http://izquotes.com/quote/334390.

37. Paul Bloom, "The Baby in the Well: The Case against Empathy," *The New Yorker*, May 20, 2013, 118–121.

38. Arjen Boin, Paul T. Hart, Allen McConnell, and Thomas Preston, "Leadership Style, Crisis Response and Blame Management: The Case of Hurricane Katrina," *Public Administration*, 88 (September 2010): 706–723.

39. Weick and Sutcliffe, *Managing the Unexpected*, 85–86.

40. Don Sands, former incident commander in oil operations, interview with author, March 25, 2015.

41. Jan Johnson, e-mail correspondence with the author, January 13, 2015.

Chapter 3

1. Janice Lachance, former head of the U.S. Office of Personnel Management, interview with author, May 13, 2014.

2. Originally the title of a poem and treatise by Saint John of the Cross in the 1570s and 1580s and subsequently adopted by Catholics and others to refer to deep spiritual anguish and crisis.

3. Alison Whitacre, construction business, interview with author, December 6, 2013.

4. Lowell Bryan and Diana Farrell, "Leading through Uncertainty," *McKinsey Quarterly* (December 2008), www.mckinsey.com/insights/managing_in_uncertainty/leading_through_uncertainty.

5. Nassim Nicholas Taleb, *The Black Swan: The Impact of the Highly Improbable* (New York: Random House, 2010).

6. Carol Tavris and Elliot Aronson, *Mistakes Were Made (but Not by Me): Why We Justify Foolish Beliefs, Bad Decisions, and Hurtful Acts* (Orlando, FL: Harcourt, 2007), 228.

7. American Psychological Association, "What Is Resilience?," *Psych Central*, 2007, http://psychcentral.com/lib/what-is-resilience/0001145.

8. Ibid.

9. Steven M. Southwick and Dennis S. Charney, *Resilience: The Science of Mastering Life's Greatest Challenges: Ten Keys to Weather and Bounce Back from Stress and Trauma* (Cambridge, MA: Cambridge University Press, 2013), 7.

10. American Psychological Association, "What Is Resilience?"

11. Karen Reivich and Andrew Shatté, *The Resilience Factor: 7 Keys to Finding Your Inner Strength and Overcoming Life's Hurdles* (New York: Three Rivers Press, 2002).

12. Ibid., 321.

13. American Psychological Association, "Recovering Emotionally from Disaster," Revised August 2013, http://www.apa.org/helpcenter/recovering-disasters.aspx.

14. Norman R. Augustine, "Managing the Crisis You Tried to Prevent," *Harvard Business Review*, November 1995.

15. Judith Rodin, *The Resilience Dividend: Being Strong in a World Where Things Go Wrong* (New York: Public Affairs, 2014).

16. Charles Perrow, *Normal Accidents: Living with High Risk Technologies* (New York: Basic Books, 1984).

17. Karl E. Weick, *Sensemaking in Organizations* (Thousand Oaks, CA: Sage, 1995).

18. Karl E. Weick and Kathleen M. Sutcliffe, *Managing the Unexpected: Assuring High Performance in an Age of Complexity* (San Francisco: Jossey-Bass, 2001), 69–70.

19. Christian Moore, with Brad Anderson and Kristin McQuivey, *The Resilience Breakthrough: 27 Tools for Turning Adversity into Action* (Austin, TX: Greenleaf Book Group Press, 2014), 174.

20. Ibid., 71.

21. Bessel van der Kolk, excerpt, ch. 13, "Healing from Trauma; Owning Your Self," from *The Body Keeps the Score: Brain, Mind, and Body in the Healing of Trauma*, in "New Ways of Treating Trauma; Try Some Yoga," *Here & Now*, January 12, 2015, hereandnow.wbur.org/2015/01/12/treating-trauma-yoga.

22. Steve Lynott, business consultant, interview with author, December 3, 2013.

23. Ginger Lew, senior advisor to the White House National Economic Council, interview with author, February 14, 2014.

24. Chesley Sullenberger, with Douglas Century, *Making a Difference: Stories of Vision and Courage from America's Leaders* (New York: Morrow, 2012), 2.

25. Steve Denne, COO, Heifer International, interview with author, January 8, 2014.

26. Russell Laine, past president, International Association of Chiefs of Police, interview with author, March 24, 2014.

27. Renae Conley, CEO of Entergy, LA, interview with author, February 14, 2014.

28. Greg Temple, business executive, interview with author, March 25, 2014.

29. Amelia Perkins, "Conversations with Nuns," *Harvard Divinity Bulletin* (Summer/Autumn 2014): 12–13.

30. Dylan Taylor, interview with author, February 11, 2014.

31. Patrice Nelson, interview with author, January 23, 2014.

32. Bill George, with Peter Sims, *True North: Discover Your Authentic Leadership* (New York: John Wiley & Sons, 2007), xxxii.

33. Augustine, "Managing the Crisis."

34. Ronald Heifetz, Alexander Grashow, and Marty Linsky, "Leadership in a (Permanent) Crisis," *Harvard Business Review*, July 2009.

35. Linda Rabbitt, founder and CEO of a construction company, interview with author, February 11, 2014.

36. Michael Dukakis, former governor of Massachusetts, interview with author, December 17, 2013.

37. Steve Piano, human resources executive, interview with author, December 16, 2013.

38. Faaiza Rashid, Amy C. Edmondson, and Herman B. Leonard, "Leadership Lessons from the Chilean Mine Rescue," *Harvard Business Review*, July 2013.

39. Stephanie Streeter, interview.

40. Anne Kemp, business consultant, interview with author, December 5, 2013.

41. James Hillman, *Kinds of Power: A Guide to Its Intelligent Uses* (New York: Currency Doubleday, 1995), 240–241.

Chapter 4

1. *How Can I Help? Stories and Reflections on Service* (New York: Knopf, 1987), 241.

2. Renae Conley interview.

3. Randall W. Helmick and John H. Zemanek, "How Entergy Battled Back-to-Back Hurricanes," *Electric Light & Power*, January 1, 2006, www.elp.com.

4. Dass and Gorman, *How Can I Help?*, 227.

5. James G. March and Mie Augier, "James March on Education, Leadership and Don Quixote: Introduction and Interview," *Academy of Management Learning & Education*, 3 (June 2004): 169–177.

6. Michael Conforti, therapist and teacher, interview with author, May 18, 2014.

7. Ben Cohen and Jerry Greenfield, interviewed by Cal Fussman, "The Ice Cream Guys," *Esquire*, January 2014, 58.

8. Jane E. Dutton, Peter J. Frost, Monica C. Worline, Jacoba M. Lilius, and Jason M. Kanov, "Leading in Times of Trauma," *Harvard Business Review*, January 2002, 58.

9. Ibid., 61.

10. Dan G. Blazer, "What Faith Communities Can Teach Psychiatrists about Depression," *Harvard Divinity Bulletin* (Summer/Autumn 2014): 10.

11. Nirmal Joshi, "Doctor, Shut Up and Listen," *New York Times*, January 4, 2015.

12. Peter D. Kramer, "Why Doctors Need Stories: In an Era of Systematic Clinical Research, Medicine Still Requires the Vignette," *New York Times*, October 19, 2014.

13. Elizabeth Bernstein, "Be There for a Friend's Relationship Crisis, but Don't Give Advice," *Wall Street Journal*, February 9, 2015.

14. Barry Dym, therapist and nonprofit leader, interview with author, December 19, 2013.

15. Denise Hudson, business executive, interview with author, January 20, 2014.

16. Greg Temple interview.

17. Bernard Rimé and Véronique Cristophe, "How Individual Emotional Episodes Feed Collective Memory," in James W. Pennebaker, Dario Paez, and Bernard Rimé, eds., *Collective Memory of Political Events: Social Psychological Perspectives* (Mahwah, NJ: Lawrence Erlbaum Associates, 1997), 133.

18. "Connecticut School Shooting: President Barack Obama Speaks at Sandy Hook Victims Vigil," *Chicago Tribune*, December 10, 2012.

19. "André Sougarret: The Brains behind the Chile Mine Rescue," October 15, 2010, antaranews.com/en/news/1287125918/andre-sougarret-the-brains-behind-the-chile-mine-rescue.

20. Frank Lloyd interview.

21. Patricia Sellers, "The Unluckiest President in America," *Fortune*, April 1, 2015, 102.

22. Ibid.

23. Kristi M. Lewis, "When Leaders Display Emotion: How Followers Respond to Negative Emotional Expression of Male and Female Leaders," *Journal of Organizational Behavior*, 21, special issue (March 2000): 221–234.

24. Ibid., 231.

25. Merlijn Venus, Daan Stam, and Daam van Knippenberg, "Leader Emotion as a Catalyst of Effective Leader Communication of Visions, Value-Laden Messages, and Goals," *Organizational Behavior and Human Decision Processes*, 122 (2013): 53.

26. Ibid., 66.

27. Ronald A. Heifetz and Marty Linsky, *Leadership on the Line: Staying Alive through the Dangers of Leading* (Cambridge, MA: Harvard Business School Press, 2002), 53.

28. Stevan E. Hobfoll et al., "Five Essential Elements of Immediate and Mid-Term Mass Trauma Intervention: Empirical Evidence," *Psychiatry*, 70 (Winter 2007): 283–315.

29. Lionel Tiger, "Hope," in Alice Rose George and Lee Marks, eds., *Hope Photographs* (New York: Thames and Hudson, 1998), 177.

30. Ibid., xiv.

31. Harry Hutson and Barbara Perry, *Putting Hope to Work: Five Principles to Activate Your Organization's Most Powerful Resource* (Westport, CT: Praeger, 2006).

32. Gabriele Oettingen, "The Problem with Positive Thinking," *New York Times*, October 26, 2014.

33. J. Edward Russo and Paul J. H. Schoemaker, "Managing Overconfidence," *Sloan Management Review* (Winter, 1992): 7–17.

34. Courtney Wilson, B&O Museum, interview with author, April 22, 2013.

35. Frederick N. Rasmussen, "Back Story: 2003 Blizzard Caused B&O Roof Collapse," *Baltimore Sun*, February 14, 2013.

36. Dass and Gorman, *How Can I Help?*, 15.

37. Ibid., 16.

Chapter 5

1. Ursula K. Le Guin, "It Was a Dark and Stormy Night; Or, Why Are We Huddling about the Campfire?" *Critical Inquiry*, 7 (Autumn, 1980): 199.

2. Howard E. Gardner, with Emma Laskin, *Leading Minds: An Anatomy of Leadership* (New York: Basic Books, 2011), 59.

3. Stephen Denning, *The Leaders' Guide to Storytelling: Mastering the Art and Discipline of Business Narrative* (San Francisco: Jossey-Bass, 2011), ix.

4. *State of the Global Workplace: Employee Engagement Insights for Business Leaders Worldwide* (n.p.: Gallup Inc., 2013).

5. Frank Kaminski, police chief, interview with author, March 16, 2014.

6. Rose Ott, investment firm officer, interview with author, March 30, 2014.

7. Dean Scarborough, CEO of Avery Dennison, interview with author, November 14, 2013.

8. Susan Carey, "Fixing a 'Fragile' Air Merger," *Wall Street Journal*, December 2, 2013.

9. Tom Yeomans, spiritual psychologist, interview with author, January 7, 2014.

10. Sarah S. M. Townsend, Dina Eliezer, and Brenda Major, "The Embodiment of Meaning Violations," in Keith D. Markham, Travis Proulx, and Matthew J. Lindberg, eds., *The Psychology of Meaning* (Washington, D.C.: American Psychological Association, 2013), 383.

11. Ibid., 319.

12. Victor E. Frankl, *Man's Search for Meaning: An Introduction to Logotherapy* (New York: Washington Square Press, 1963), 121.

13. Travis Proulx, Keith D. Markham, and Matthew J. Lindberg, "Introduction: The New Science of Meaning," in Keith D. Markham et al., eds., *The Psychology of Meaning*, 383.

14. Ronnie Janoff-Bulman, *Shattered Assumptions: Towards a New Psychology of Trauma* (New York: Free Press, 1992), 6–10.

15. Ibid., 19.

16. Barry Dym, interview.

17. Travis Proulx and Micheal Inzlicht, "The Five 'A's of Meaning Maintenance: Finding Meaning in the Theories of Sense-Making," *Psychological Inquiry: An International Journal for the Advancement of Psychological Theory*, 23, no. 4 (2012): 317–335.

18. George E. Vaillant, "Ego Mechanisms of Defense and Personality Psychopathology," *Journal of Abnormal Psychology*, 103, no. 1 (1994): 44–50.

19. Janoff-Bulman, *Shattered Assumptions*, 141.

20. Russell Laine, interview.

21. Dan P. McAdams, "Leaders and Their Life Stories: Obama, Bush, and Narratives of Redemption," in George R. Goethals, Scott T. Allison, Roderick M. Kramer, and David M. Messick, eds., *Conceptions of Leadership: Enduring Ideas and Emerging Insights* (New York: Palgrave Macmillan, 2014), 148.

22. Ibid.

23. Dan P. McAdams, *The Redemptive Self: Stories Americas Live By* (New York: Oxford University Press, 2013), xiv.

24. George Graves, police chief, interview with author, March 4, 2014.

25. Stephen Joseph, *What Doesn't Kill Us: The New Psychology of Posttraumatic Growth* (New York: Basic Books, 2011), 131.

26. Karl E. Weick, *Sensemaking in Organizations* (Thousand Oaks, CA: Sage, 1995), 60–61.

27. Melanie C. Green, "Research Statement," University of North Carolina, wunc.edu, 2012, 2.

28. Norman K. Denzin, *Performance Ethnography: Critical Pedagogy and the Politics of Culture* (Thousand Oaks, CA: Sage, 2003), 234.

29. Green, "Research Statement," 2.

30. Hannah B. Harvey, *The Art of Storytelling: From Parents to Professionals*, Course Guidebook (Chantilly, VA: Great Courses, 2013), 5–6.

31. Jenna L. Clark, Melanie C. Green, and Joseph J.P. Simons, "Narrative Warmth and Quantitative Competence: Message Type Affects Impressions of a Speaker," University of North Carolina at Chapel Hill and Institute for High Performance Computing, Singapore, January 15, 2014. Unpublished draft.

32. Robin L. Nabi and Melanie C. Green, "The Role of a Narrative's Emotional Flow in Promoting Persuasive Outcomes," *Media Psychology*, 2014, 1, doi: 10.1080/15213269.2014.912585, 16.

33. Gardner, *Leading Minds*, 136.

34. Paul J. Zak, "Why Your Brain Loves Good Storytelling," *Harvard Business Review* blog, October 28, 2014, www.hbr.org/2014/10why-your-brain-loves -good-storytelling/.

35. Ibid.

36. Paul J. Zak, "Why Inspiring Stories Make Us React: The Neuroscience of Narrative," *Cerebrum* (February 2015): 10.

37. Herminia Ibarra, "The Authenticity Paradox: Why Feeling Like a Fake Can Be a Sign of Growth," *Harvard Business Review*, January–February, 2015, 59.

38. Jonathan Gottschall, *The Storytelling Animal: How Stories Make Us Human* (Boston, MA: Houghton Mifflin, 2012), 197.

39. Yusufi Vali, executive director of Boston Islamic Cultural Center, interview with author, February 7, 2014.

40. Yusufi Vali, "As I See It: From Kansas City to the Boston Marathon Tragedy," *Kansas City Star*, April 8, 2014.

41. Harvey, *The Art of Storytelling*, 15.

42. "William James," *Stanford Encyclopedia of Philosophy*, September 7, 2000, 462.

43. Lani Peterson, interview.

44. Jerome Bruner, *Making Stories: Law, Literature, Life* (Cambridge, MA: Harvard University Press, 2002), 17.

45. Jerome Bruner, *Acts of Meaning* (Cambridge: Harvard University Press, 1990), 77–79.

46. Yusufi Vali, interview with author, May 14, 2015.

47. Yiannis Gabriel, "The Narrative Veil: Truth and Untruths in Storytelling," in Yiannis Gabriel, ed., *Myths, Stories, and Organizations: Premodern Narratives for Our Times* (New York: Oxford University Press, 2004), 25.

48. Geoffrey Himes, "Rosanne Cash on Discovering New Artistic Terrain: The Singer-Songwriter Looked to Her Southern Ancestors to Come Up with a Different Kind of Concept Album," *Smithsonian Magazine*, November 2014, 65.

49. Bruner, *Acts of Meaning*, 83.

50. Steve Denne, interview.

51. Marshall Ganz, "Leading Change: Leadership, Organization, and Social Movements," in Nitin Nohria and Rakesh Khurana, eds., *Handbook of Leadership Theory and Practice: An HBS Centennial Colloquium on Advancing Leadership* (Boston, MA: Harvard Business Press, 2010), 542.

52. Bernard Rimé and Véronique Christophe, "How Individual Emotional Episodes Feed Collective Memory," in James W. Pennebaker, Dario Paez, and Bernard Rimé, eds., *Collective Memory of Political Events: Social Psychological Perspectives* (Mahwah, NJ: Lawrence Erlbaum Associates, 1997), 144.

53. Gardner, *Acts of Meaning*, 277.

54. Mary Jo Hatch, Monika Kostera, and Andrzej Koźmiński, *The Three Faces of Leadership: Manager, Artist, Priest* (Malden, MA: Blackwell Publishing, 2005), 42.

55. Karl E. Weick and Kathleen M. Sutcliffe, *Managing the Unexpected: Assuring High Performance in an Age of Complexity* (San Francisco: Jossey-Bass, 2001), 167.

56. Dario Paez, Nekane Basabe, and Jose Luis Gonzalez, "Social Processes and Collective Memory: A Cross-Cultural Approach to Remembering Political Events," in James W. Pennebaker et al., eds., *Collective Memory*, 147–174.

Chapter 6

1. Tony Hoagland, "Bible Study," *Poetry CCV*, March 2015, 521.

2. Jerome Bruner, *Making Stories: Law, Literature, Life* (Cambridge, MA: Harvard University Press, 2002), 20.

3. Jeff Share, "How Rod West Overcame the Challenge from Hell," *Pipeline and Gas Journal* 237 (September 2010).

4. Rod West, business executive, interviews with author, January 24, 2014, and September 24, 2014.

5. Kensington Duncan, "How Much Damage Did Hurricane Katrina Cause?," February 18, 2013, http://disasterandemergencysurvival.com/archives/how-much-damage-did-hurricane-katrina-cause. Retrieved May 25, 2015.

6. Share, "How Rod West Overcame."

7. Judith Rodin, *The Resilience Dividend: Being Strong in a World Where Things Go Wrong* (New York: Public Affairs, 2014), 236, 251, 268, 273.

Chapter 7

1. Kale Garcia, interview.

2. Josh Gotbaum, "How Amtrak Failed the Victims of Train 188: A Survivor's Tale," *Politico*, May 19, 2015.

3. Ibid.

4. Ibid.

5. Lisa Feldman Barrett, "Valence Is a Basic Building Block of Emotional Life," *Journal of Research in Personality*, 40 (2006): 35–50.

6. Jerome S. Bruner and Leo Postman, "On the Perception of Incongruity: A Paradigm," *Journal of Personality*, 18 (1949): 206–223.

7. Ibid., 218.

8. Ibid., 208.

9. Michael Conforti, "Memories, Trauma, and Healing," Part 3 in lecture series, December 2, 2013.

10. American Psychological Association, "Trauma," apa.org/topics/trauma/index.aspx.

11. American Psychological Association, "Recovering Emotionally from Disaster," apa.org/helpcenter/recovering-disasters.aspx.

12. Stephen Joseph, *What Doesn't Kill Us: The New Psychology of Posttraumatic Growth* (New York: Basic Books, 2011), 21–47.

13. Michael Conforti, "Memories, Trauma, and Healing," Part 4 in lecture series, December 9, 2013.

14. Michael Conforti, December 2, 2013.

15. American Psychological Association, "Post-traumatic Stress Disorder," apa.org/topics/ptsd/index.aspx.

16. David Finkel, "The Return: The Traumatized Veterans of Iraq and Afghanistan," *New Yorker*, September 9, 2013, 36–40.

17. Gregg Zeroya, "Report: Military Efforts to Prevent Mental Illness Ineffective," *USA Today*, February 20, 2014.

18. Stefanie Pidgeon, "Army's First Executive Resilience, Performance Course Offered to Army Leaders at Belvoir," published October 21, 2013, army.mil/ article/113437/Army_s_first_Executive_Resilience_Performance_Course_offered _to_Army_leaders_at_Belvoir/.

19. Finkel, "The Return," 36.

20. W. Brad Johnson, Michael Bertschinger, Alicia Snell, and Amber Wilson, "Secondary Trauma and Ethical Obligations for Military Psychologists: Preserving Compassion and Competence in the Crucible of Combat," *Psychological Services*, 11 (February 2014): 68–74.

21. Jeneen Interlandi, "How Do You Heal a Traumatized Mind?" *New York Times Magazine*, May 25, 2014, 42–58.

22. George A. Bonanno, Chris R. Brewin, Krysztof Kaniasty, and Annett M. La Greca, "Weighing the Costs of Disaster: Consequences, Risks, and Resilience in Individuals, Families, and Communities," *Psychological Science in the Public Interest*, 11, no. 1 (2010): 2.

23. Patrick O'Malley, "Getting Grief Right," *New York Times*, January 11, 2015.

24. Timothy D. Wilson, Dieynaba G. Ndiaye, Cheryl Hahn, and Daniel T. Gilbert, "Still a Thrill: Meaning Making and the Pleasures of Uncertainty," in Keith D. Markman, Travis Proulx, and Matthew J. Lindberg, eds., *The Psychology of Meaning* (Washington, D.C.: American Psychological Association, 2013), 437.

25. Bonanno et al., "Weighing the Costs," 1–49.

26. George Bonanno, premier date June 10, 2013, http://www.tc.columbia/ edu/admin/125/moments.asp?id=9069.

27. Lawrence G. Calhoun and Richard G. Tedeschi, "The Foundations of Traumatic Growth: New Considerations," *Psychological Inquiry: An International Journal for the Advancement of Psychological Theory* (2004): 93–102.

28. Conforti, December 9, 2013.

29. Mark Miller, "Surviving the Jolt," *AARP: The Magazine*, April–May 2014, 80.

30. Calhoun and Tedeschi, "The Foundations," 93–102.

31. Lawrence G. Calhoun and Richard G. Tedeschi, *Posttraumatic Growth in Clinical Practice* (New York: Routledge, 2013).

32. Richard G. Tedeschi, Lawrence G. Calhoun, and Lynne Cooper, "Rumination and Posttraumatic Growth in Older Adults," Paper presented at the meeting of the American Psychological Association, Washington, D.C., August 2000.

33. Sarah S. M. Townsend, Dina Eliezer, and Brenda Major, "The Embodiment of Meaning Violations," in Markman et al., *The Psychology of Meaning*, 383.

34. Wyatt Mason, "You Are Not Alone across Time: Using Sophocles to Treat PTSD," *Harper's Magazine*, October 2014, 57–65.

35. Ibid., 65.

36. Victor Frankl, *The Doctor and the Soul, from Psychotherapy to Logotherapy* (New York: Random House, 1986), 67–68.

37. Jennifer L. Pals and Dan P. McAdams, "The Transformed Self: A Narrative Understanding of Posttraumatic Growth," *Psychological Inquiry*, 15, no. 1 (2004): 65.

38. Dan P. McAdams, "How Actors, Agents and Authors Find Meaning in Life," in Markman et al., *The Psychology of* Meaning, 180.

39. Max DePree, *Leadership Is an Art* (New York: Dell Publishing, 1989), 91–92.

40. William F. Breisch and Martin G. Lexmond, "An Examination of the Phenomenon of Growth after Trauma and Its Influence on Leadership," Dissertation presented in partial fulfillment of the requirements for the Doctor of Education degree in Leadership for the Advancement of Learning and Service, College of Education and Leadership, Cardinal Stritch University, May 2013.

41. Harry Schlough, business executive, interview with author, April 3, 2014.

42. Charlotte Walker, entrepreneur and business executive, interview with author, December 4, 2013.

43. Zoltan Csimma, human resources executive, interview with author, February 6, 2014.

44. Breisch and Lexmond, "An Examination," 12.

45. Jefferson A. Singer, "Narrative Identity and Meaning Making across the Adult Lifespan: An Introduction," *Journal of Personality*, 72 (June 2004): 446.

46. Roxane Cohen Silver and John A. Updegraff, "Searching for and Finding Meaning Following Personal and Collective Traumas," in Markman et al., *The Psychology of* Meaning, 247.

47. Ibid., 248.

48. Ibid., 249.

49. Ibid.

50. Pals and McAdams, "The Transformed Self," 67.

51. Tom Yeomans, interview.

52. Kathryn Schulz, *Being Wrong: Adventures in the Margin of Error* (New York: Ecco, 2010), 6.

53. Ron Heifetz R., Alexander Grashow A., and Marty Linsky, "Leadership in a (Permanent) Crisis," *Harvard Business Review*, July 2009.

54. Patrick T. Reardon, "John Barth Muses on Stories, Readers, a Splendid Pen," *Chicago Tribune*, January 2, 2006.

Recommended References

Barton, Laurence. *Crisis Leadership Now: A Real-World Guide to Preparing for Threats, Disaster, Sabotage, and Scandal.* New York: McGraw-Hill, 2008.

Bion, Wilfred R., *Experiences in Groups and Other Papers.* New York: Basic Books, 1961.

Bruner, Jerome. *Acts of Meaning.* Cambridge, MA: Harvard University Press, 1990.

Bruner, Jerome. *Making Stories: Law, Literature, Life.* Cambridge, MA: Harvard University Press, 2002.

Calhoun, Lawrence G. and Richard G. Tedeschi. *Posttraumatic Growth in Clinical Practice.* New York: Routledge, 2013.

Dass, Ram, and Paul Gorman. *How Can I Help? Stories and Reflections on Service.* New York: Knopf, 1987.

Feldman, David B. and Lee Daniel Kravetz. *Supersurvivors: The Surprising Link between Suffering and Success.* New York: HarperCollins, 2014.

Fink, Steven. *Crisis Management: Planning for the Inevitable.* New York: AMACOM, 1986.

Frankl, Victor. *The Doctor and the Soul: From Psychotherapy to Logotherapy.* New York: Vintage, 1973.

Frankl, Victor E. *Man's Search for Meaning: An Introduction to Logotherapy.* New York: Washington Square Press, 1963.

Gabriel, Yiannis, ed. *Myths, Stories, and Organizations: Premodern Narratives for Our Times.* New York: Oxford, 2004.

Gardner, Howard. With Emma Laskin. *Leading Minds: An Anatomy of Leadership.* New York: Basic Books, 2011.

George, Bill. With Peter Sims. *True North: Discover Your Authentic Leadership.* San Francisco, CA: Jossey-Bass, 2007.

Goethals, George R., Scott T. Allison, Roderick M. Kramer, and David M. Messick, eds. *Conceptions of Leadership: Enduring Ideas and Emerging Insights*. New York: Palgrave Macmillan, 2014.

Goffman, Erving. *The Presentation of Self in Everyday Life*. Garden City, NY: Anchor, 1959.

Gonzales, Laurence. *Deep Survival: Who Lives, Who Dies, and Why*. New York: W. W. Norton & Company, 2003.

Gottschall, Jonathan. *The Storytelling Animal: How Stories Make Us Human*. Boston, MA: Mariner Books, 2012.

Greenleaf, Robert K. *Servant Leadership: A Journey into the Nature of Legitimate Power and Greatness*. New York: Paulist Press, 1991.

Harvard Business Review. *Harvard Business Review on Crisis Management*. Boston, MA: Harvard Business School Press, 2000.

Harvey, Hannah B. *The Art of Story-Telling: From Parents to Professionals*. Chantilly, VA: The Great Courses, 2013.

Heifetz, Ronald. *Leadership without Easy Answers*. Cambridge, MA: Harvard University Press, 1994.

Heifetz, Ronald A., and Marty Linsky. *Leadership on the Line: Staying Alive through the Dangers of Leading*. Boston, MA: Harvard Business School, 2002.

Hopper, Earl, ed. *Trauma and Organizations*. London: Karnac, 2012.

Hutson, Harry, and Barbara Perry. *Putting Hope to Work: Five Principles to Activate Your Organization's Most Powerful Resource*. Westport, CT: Praeger, 2006.

James, Erika Hayes, and Lynn Perry Wooten. *Leading under Pressure: From Surviving to Thriving before, during, and after a Crisis*. New York: Routledge, 2010.

Janoff-Bulman, Ronnie. *Shattered Assumptions: Towards a New Psychology of Trauma*. New York: Free Press, 1992.

Johnson, Martha. *On My Watch: Leadership, Innovation, and Personal Resilience*. Sonoita, AZ: Dudley Court Press, 2013.

Joseph, Stephen. *What Doesn't Kill Us: The New Psychology of Posttraumatic Growth*. New York: Basic Books, 2011.

Lewis, Gerald. *Organizational Crisis Management: The Human Factor*. Boca Raton, FL: Auerbach Publication, 2006.

Markman, Keith D., Travis Proulx, and Matthew J. Lindberg, eds. *The Psychology of Meaning*. Washington, D.C.: American Psychological Association, 2013.

McAdams, Dan P. *The Redemptive Self: Stories Americans Live By*. New York: Oxford, 2013.

Mitroff, Ian I. *Why Some Companies Emerge Stronger and Better from a Crisis: 7 Essential Lessons for Surviving Disaster*. New York: AMACOM, 2005.

Moore, Christian. *The Resilience Break-Through: 27 Tools for Turning Adversity into Action*. Austin, TX: Greenleaf Book Group, 2014.

Nohria, Nitin, and Rakesh Khurana, eds. *Handbook of Leadership Theory and Practice: An HBS Colloquium on Advancing Leadership*. Boston, MA: Harvard Business Press, 2010.

Power, Mick, and Chris R. Brewin, eds. *The Transformation of Meaning in Psychological Therapies: Integrating Theory and Practice.* New York: John Wiley and Sons, 1997.

Reivich, Karen, and Andrew Shatté. *The Resilience Factor: 7 Keys to Finding Your Inner Strength and Overcoming Life's Hurdles.* New York: Three Rivers Press, 2002.

Rodin, Judith. *The Resilience Dividend: Being Strong in a World Where Things Go Wrong.* New York: Public Affairs, 2014.

Schulz, Kathryn. *Being Wrong: Adventures in the Margin of Error.* New York: Ecco, 2010.

Southwick, Steven M., and Dennis S. Charney. *Resilience: The Science of Mastering Life's Greatest Challenges.* New York: Cambridge University Press, 2012.

Sullenberger, Chesley. With Douglas Century. *Making a Difference: Stories of Vision and Courage from America's Leaders.* New York: Harper Collins, 2012.

Taleb, Nassim Nicholas. *The Black Swan: The Impact of the Highly Improbable.* New York: Random House, 2010.

Tavris, Carol, and Elliot Aronson. *Mistakes Were Made (but Not By Me): Why We Justify Foolish Beliefs, Bad Decisions, and Hurtful Acts.* New York: Harcourt, 2008.

Weick, Karl E. *Sensemaking in Organizations.* Thousand Oaks, CA: Sage Publications, 1995.

Weick, Karl E., and Kathleen M. Sutcliffe. *Managing the Unexpected: Assuring High Performance in an Age of Complexity.* San Francisco, CA: Jossey-Bass, 2001.

Weiss, Tzipi, and Ron Berger, eds. *Posttraumatic Growth and Culturally Competent Practice: Lessons Learned from around the Globe.* Hoboken, NJ: John Wiley and Sons, 2010.

Index

About the Authors

Harry Hutson, PhD, is an independent consultant who coaches leaders, designs and delivers leadership development initiatives, and writes about leadership. He has held executive roles in four multinational corporations and teaching roles in several universities. His books include *Leadership in Nonprofit Organizations: Lessons from the Third Sector* (with Barry Dym) and *Putting Hope to Work: Five Principles to Activate Your Organization's Most Powerful Resource* (with Barbara Perry). Hutson holds degrees from Hamilton College, Harvard Divinity School, Stanford University, and Indiana University. His web address is www.harryhutson.com.

Martha Johnson, MBA, is an author, speaker, and consultant with a 35-year career in public and private organizations. She served President Obama as the Administrator of the General Services Administration. She also served eight years with the Clinton Administration. Her business career includes senior positions at Cummins Engine Company, Computer Sciences Corporation, SRA International, and the Boston architecture firm, Ellenzweig. Her published work includes *On My Watch: Leadership, Innovation, and Personal Resilience*, an Amazon best seller in 2013, and a novel, *In Our Midst*. Johnson holds degrees from Oberlin College and Yale University. She blogs at www.MarthaJohnson.com.